&\also

hawkins\brown

Black Dog Publishing
London/New York

BOOKS READ ARE NEVER RIGHT ORDER IN THE.

Introduction
Rowan Moore

Architects have different ways of naming themselves. Some go for the suggestive/shocking/enigmatic/typographically challenging collective noun: BaRfF, or the like. Others choose strings of letters denoting suave corporate anonymity. Then there is the plain, honest formula of Ordinary Name/Ordinary Name. Or Ordinary Name/Ordinary Name/Ordinary Name. Hawkins\Brown, but for that cute reverse slash between the names, are clearly in the latter category.

The O.N./O.N. formula tends to belong to practices formed in the late 1980s, a time when ideology had been officially abolished, along with public patronage and community. Architects then were apologetic for the sins of a previous generation, their defensive reflexes well-developed in the face of a rampant Prince of Wales and professional indemnity horror stories. Such practices developed certain priorities: serve the client; achieve quality; try and be a bit contemporary if you can. From this followed a careful modernism typified by plain rectangles of whiteness+colour+glass+nice wood or stone.

At first sight Hawkins\Brown belong squarely in this tradition. The prosperous busy hum that emanates from their office is that of one that serves clients and keeps the rain out. There are a lot of plain rectangles in their work. So it comes as a surprise to find a book like this about them, one with a whiff of Rem Koolhaas and his S,M,L,XL in its promiscuous interleaving of diverse graphic material and its forays into anti-glamourous photography. Isn't this a bit pretentious, you wonder, for such a no-nonsense practice?

But then a little bell goes off in the brain of the formerly inattentive critic. It is the same bell that went off when he heard that Hawkins\Brown were designing Rachel Whiteread's house. The first thought was: "shouldn't she commission a more ostentiously cool practice, given her status as the patron saint of happening architects?" Then, however, he wonders whether she hadn't actually spotted something in them

beyond the deceptive surface appearance. Perhaps it is not quite adequate to pigeonhole Hawkins\Brown as tasteful pragmatists. Damn, goes the critic, I am going to have to think a little harder about these people!

And, indeed, they are not just about nice materials and careful details. There is something distinctive about their work, which might be described as the power of the telling fact, expressed with good-humoured energy. An example is the Women's Pioneer Housing Headquarters. Next to a railway line, the structure had to be installed without disrupting the existing offices underneath, which leads to some simple decisions. It is a box, easy to make with a steel frame, with wooden cladding that matches the robust setting, but also softens it. The roof is made of grass to improve the views from overlooking flats, and windows are angled to catch views and light. So far so logical, except that the addition of these decisions creates something unexpected. It is a portakabin, but not as we know it. You can't argue with it, but it is surprising. A+B=Q, or as Hawkins\Brown put it &\also.

Once you've spotted this sensibility, you see it everywhere, including works like the Playbarn, and the meteorites rising outside Centre Point. They are pretty much the shapes they need to be, which happen to be intriguing ones. Other architects design things that look not dissimilar, but few can match Hawkins\Brown's particular allergy to aesthetic flummery, or to elaboration. These buildings have strong personalities, but there is no irritating ego, and no preciousness, interposing itself between the building, its use, and its users.

This is particularly true of the Bradbury Street market stalls. This project takes an eternal high tech fantasy, that of the industrially produced unit delivered whole to site, and puts it to practical use. Normally such fantasies have a problem when they come into contact with reality, as the architect's dreams of something like a racing yacht encounter a situation where a skip would be more appropriate. Not here. The prefabricated market stalls are well-made and striking, but they also have the requisite toughness, and something about them that accommodates stacked-up piles of toilet paper and bleach bottles without looking bad. In fact they look better. These are not structures that need to be photographed in crisp early morning sunlight, with a diligent assistant clearing away the messy stuff.

Hawkins\Brown's buildings are about life as it is lived, particularly in urban London, particularly to the north and east of the city. Because the buildings are so direct, they communicate directly. They need no special explanations. Everyone can see what they are for and what they do. They have pursued this theme persistently for 15 years, and have built up an impressive body of work.

There is no reason why they should not continue in the same vein for another 15 years, and another, but there is a sense in this book that they might want to try out a few other things too. There is an intriguing image in their project for a Maggie's Cancer Care Centre in Sheffield, in which the Long Library at Sissinghurst has been annotated with simple phrases such as "office space", "views out", "kitchen table", etc.. These phrases can denote the most dismally utilitarian of architectural elements, but over this interior they are sensual and richly associative.

This drawing is simply suggesting that the same could be true of the ordinary elements of the Maggie's Centre. Other commentators have said that Hawkins\Brown's buildings aim to "nurture" their inhabitants. These straightforward intentions are actually difficult to achieve in new buildings, and the hard-edged architecture of Hawkins\Brown does not always meet these goals. But just having such ambitions already sets them apart from much of their profession. Fulfilling them is a good way of spending the next decade and a half.

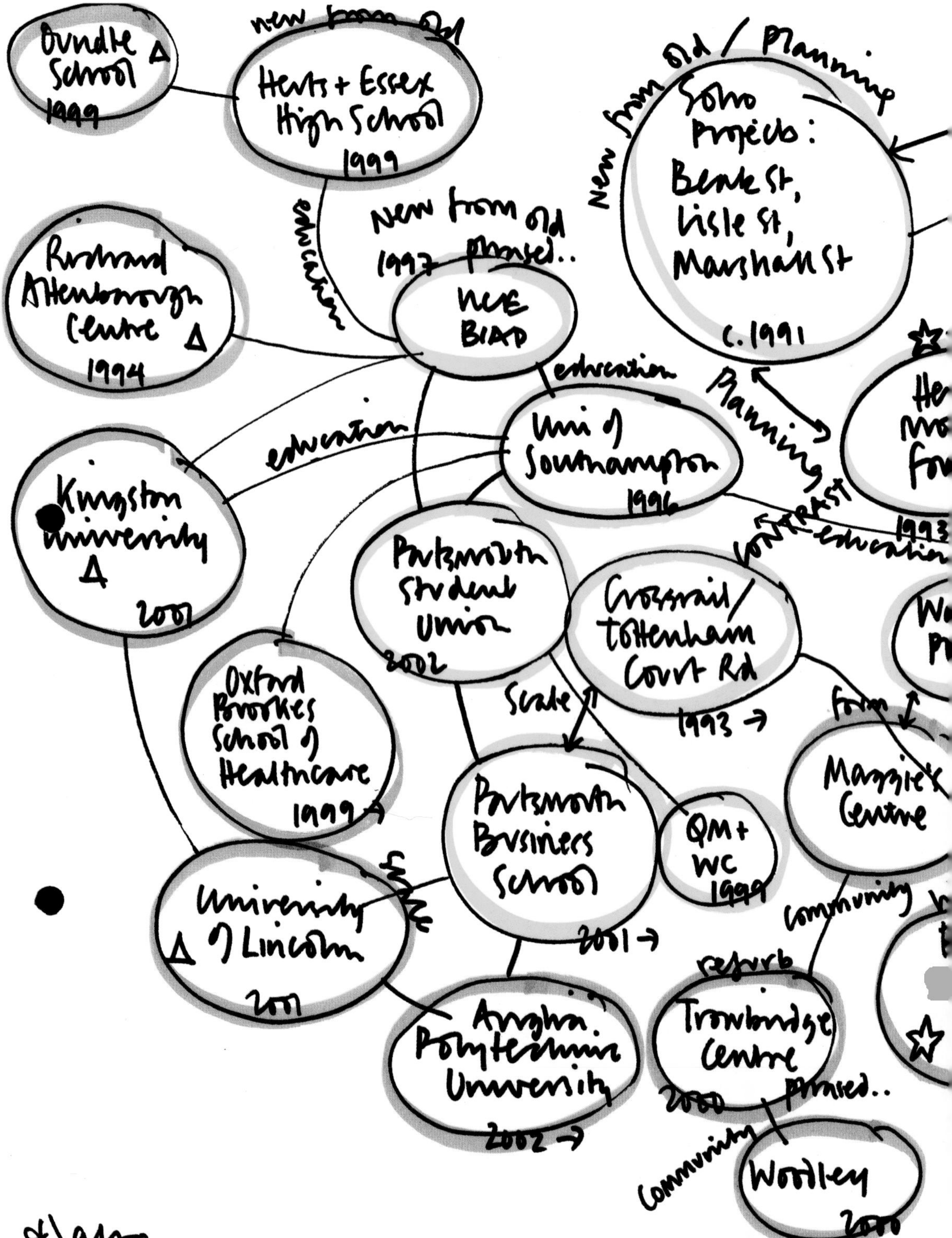

Oundle School 1999 △

Herts + Essex High School 1999

new from old

Soho Projects: Berwk St, Lisle St, Marshall St c.1991

Old / Planning

New from Old

New from old 1997 Phased...

NUE BIAD

education

Richard Attenborough Centre △ 1994

education

Uni of Southampton 1996

education

Planning

He Mo fou 1993

education

Kingston University △ 2001

education

contrast

Portsmouth Student Union 2002

Crossrail / Tottenham Court Rd 1993 →

W P

Oxford Brookes School of Healthcare 1999 →

Scale

form

Maggie's Centre

Portsmouth Business School 2001 →

QM + WC 1999

community

University △ of Lincoln 2001

scale

Anglia Polytechnic University 2002 →

reforb

Trowbridge Centre 2000

phased...

community

Woolley 2010

community

&/also

diagram of cross fertilization

☆ AWARD   △ UNREALISED   A   B   C

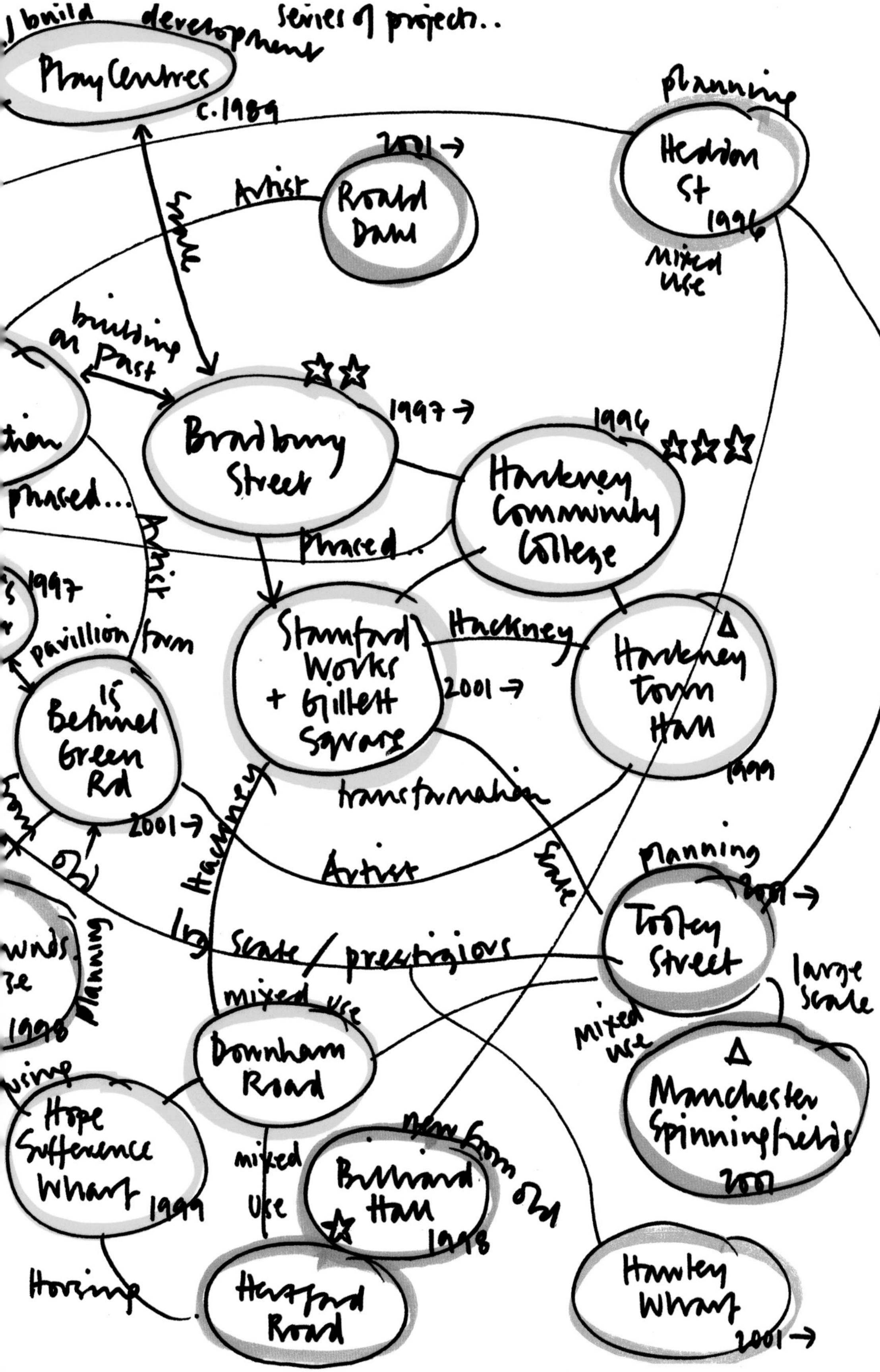

build   development   series of projects...

Play Centres
c.1989

planning

Hedson St 1996
mixed use

2001 →
Roald Dahl

Artist

same

building on Past

☆☆
Bradbury Street
1997 →

1996 ☆☆☆
Hackney Community College

...tion
phased...

1997

Artist

Phased...

Stamford Works + Gillett Square
Hackney
2001 →

△
Hackney Town Hall
1999

pavillion farm

15 Bethnal Green Rd

2001 →

Hackney

transformation

Artist

State

planning
2001 →
Totey Street

large scale

large scale / prestigious

mixed use

mixed use

△
Manchester Spinningfields
2007

...wds. ...3e
1998
planning

...sive
Hope Sufference Wharf 1999

Downham Road

mixed use

mean from old

☆
Billiard Hall
1998

Housing

Hertford Road

Hawley Wharf
2001 →

TURN THE PAGES WEARING ONE GLOVE, PREFERABLY ASBESTOS.

COFFEE TABLE? DINING TABLE? BEDSIDE TABLE? CHOOSE ONE NOW!

TRY NOT TO THINK OF A KETTLE WHILE YOU EXAMINE THIS BUILDING.

FORGET SPELLING, GRAMMAR, SYNTAX, WIT, VOCABULARY AND PUNCTUATION

. PICTURES RULE.

1
home

lent Centre
ersity of Portsmouth

sculpture advertises the new
venue and student union.

:ops are banned at Bastwick St;
ojects have a parent;
:hing leads to another;
ing just happens;
ything's connected;
vant buildings to be alive[1];
luence people;

nt Centre, University of Portsmouth;
pe to slot in a gig;

Hawkins\Brown is tidy messy;
two opposite ideas;
held in the head at the same time[1];
yet still it functions;
god bless friction;
for it drives a project;
like a film;
contrasting views both upheld;
creativity happens at loggerheads[2];

[1]Sign of first rate intelligence;
F Scott Fitzgerald;
The Crack Up;

[2]Artists need to act against something;
Jean Miro;
Had his work started by outsiders;
He painted as a reaction to this;

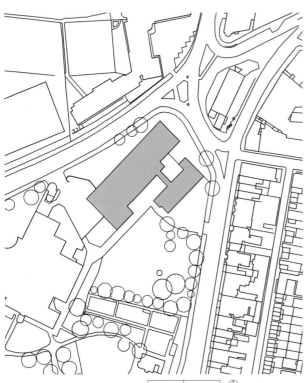

Portsmouth Students Union Site Plan 0   50m

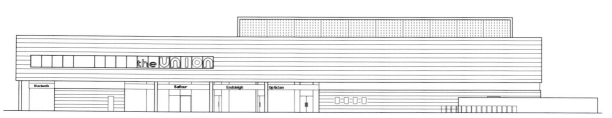

Northwest Elevation

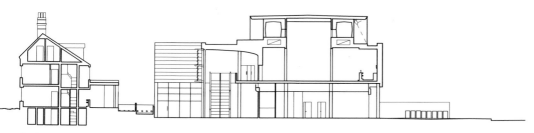

Section through Nightclub

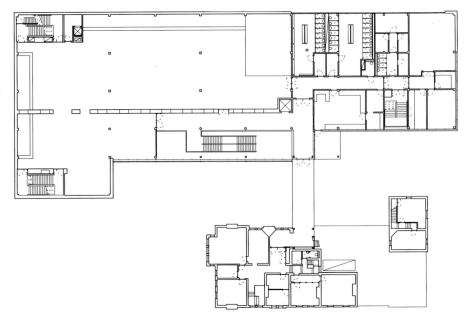

First Floor Plan

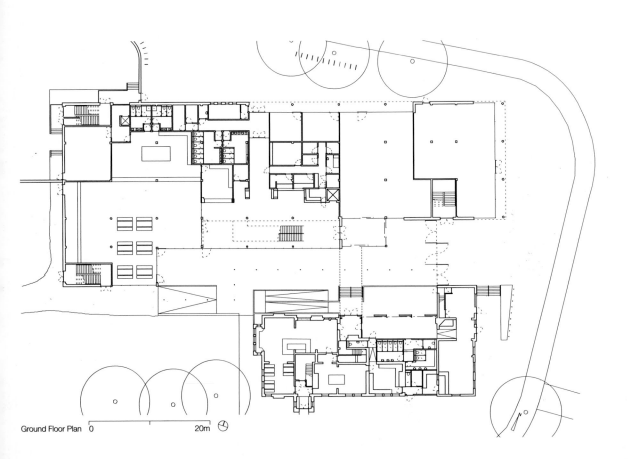

Ground Floor Plan 0   20m

TO OVERCOME READER'S BLOCK, LOOK AT THE WORDS AS PICTURES AND READ THE PHOTOGRAPHS.

Bastwick St is a goldfish square;
surrounded by light;
4 walls to stare out of;
to daydream through;
as a designer without light;
is a battery architect;
boshing out the banal;
instead of the ebullient;
the radiant;
and the funny;

worditecture;
the words that describe what we do;
what we make;
read our buildings;
in your own words;
short stories, jokes[1], poems;
a novel or two perhaps;
a song for every site;
bibliography;
discography;

[1]What's red and invisible;
No tomatoes;

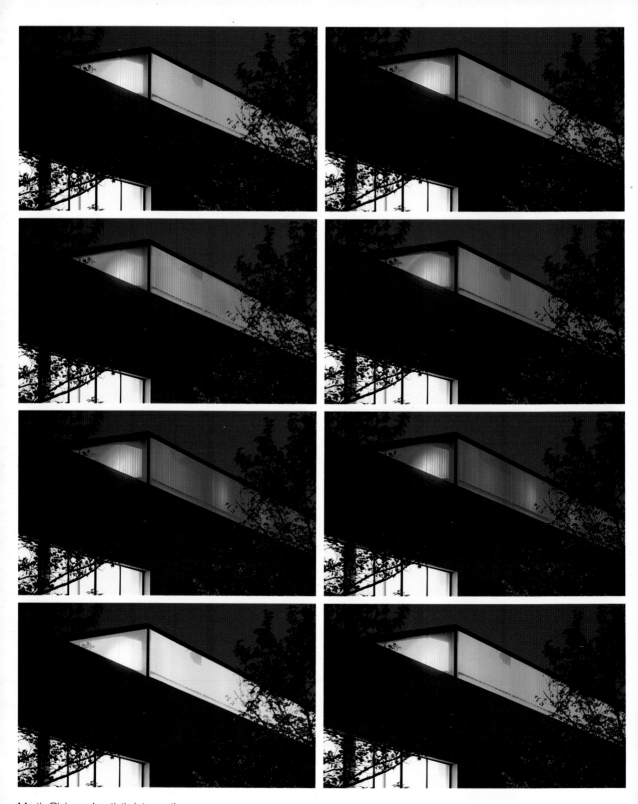

Martin Richman's artistic intervention
advertises the presence of the nightclub
inside through a changing light sculpture
on the roof

NO-ONE EVER PUT UP A STATUE OF AN ARCHITECTURAL CRITIC.

**Hawkins\Brown Studio
60 Bastwick St,
London EC1**

it's a calm office;
but not quiet;
now and again;
a director shouts his head off;
a few thousand watts of anger;
Lemmy-esque;
to punctuate serenity[1];
then ease back into his Maui shirt;
noise is essential;
to shift cobwebbed heads;
reduce mental cholesterol;
call Dr Brown;

[1]A former synagogue;
Bethnal Green Road;
Now family home, studio and box of light to one of Britain's
leading sculptors;

too much time sitting;
every 20 minutes move;
a lap of the floor;
up and down the stairs;
round the block;
call it archi-motion;
call it movement;
feel unstuckness;
walking's our jab;
against designer's block;

The traces of the relationships people make with one another…
Jane Rendell

Some time in the mid 1990s, I went to visit a friend doing research at the Sociology Department of the University of Southampton. My friend was not fond of much contemporary architecture, finding it cold and arrogant, but he wanted to show me a new building on the campus that he had already grown fond of. It had only been completed a few months previously, but despite its newness and the use of quite raw materials – unpainted concrete and steel – the building had a comfortable atmosphere. Even early on a Saturday morning, it was full of students. It already felt lived-in. It wasn't until several years later, when I was asked to write a piece on the architecture of Hawkins\Brown, that I realised this was one of their buildings.

The artist and critic Suzanne Lacy has suggested with reference to 'new genre public art' that artists can adopt a range of activities in the process of making art and that audiences are composed of people, each with their own relationship to the final work. This notion of art as a social process and one that is negotiated differently by each person involved, provides an interesting starting point for considering the various interactions in architectural practice between architect, funder, client, occupier and the building. When I asked the directors of Hawkins\Brown what their architecture meant to them, instead of describing a series of objects, they told me stories about the people they had worked with. For Hawkins\Brown "architecture has layers of meaning": the same building is understood differently by each individual involved with it.

A discussion of Hawkins\Brown's architecture raises a number of issues that are paralleled in recent theory, in particular the turn to 'space' in the late 1980s and early 90s. Cultural geographers, such as Edward Soja and Doreen Massey, have described the relationship between society and space as two-way – we make spaces and spaces make us. Architecture is at once a trace of the interactions people make with one another and their surroundings, but it also forms and transforms us both personally and socially. Architecture occupies a pivotal position temporally; on the one hand, buildings are accretions of social processes that have already taken place; on the other, they are catalysts for future action.

To negotiate the territory between theory and practice is no easy task, but I believe this to be the role of the contemporary critic. The theoretical ideas that I am interested in exploring here do not seek to prove a hypothesis or 'test' a theory in the manner of a scientific experiment. For me, theoretical work provides something else – a chance to reflect, not simply to contemplate, but instead to use the imagination to seek to change the world. Rather than take examples of architecture as illustrations of theoretical positions or apply theoretical insights retrospectively to modes of practice, I construct the relationship between theoretical concepts and architectural objects and processes though conversations. The theoretical ideas I refer to in relation to Hawkins\Brown's work are not ones that they have used to generate their architecture. This is not the point. Instead, I hope the following dialogues and my theorised reflections upon them open up a new way of understanding Hawkins\Brown's architecture, so shifting the position their practice occupies in architectural criticism in some way.

I don't seek to be an apologist for a certain kind of practice nor am I interested in choosing to study only the sort of architecture that 'matches up' to my own agenda. Instead, I am fascinated by the way in which the critic adopts a particular standpoint in relation to artists, architects and the objects and situations they create. Perhaps it is my background in architectural design that has had a spatial effect on how I think and write about art and architecture. I tend to think of criticism as a form of site-specific writing or 'situated practice'. This kind of spatial writing starts to question the distinctions made between art, architecture and theory. What I am after is the production of a certain kind of 'scene', a place where, through dialogue, conversation and exchange, new ideas and ways of considering architecture and art can be invented.

Paying attention to the particular distance that a critic adopts in relation to a work of art or architecture, an artist or an architect, gets us beyond simplistic notions of judgement and objectivity, and asks us to take seriously the very act of negotiating our position. Here we can consider the subjective and the intimate, as well as the different ways in which we look, from scrutinising close-ups to sideways glances, and talk, from prepared speeches to casual remarks made in passing. This is why, for me, conversing while moving through their work has been the most fruitful way to engage with Hawkins\Brown's architecture. The architectural critic all too often focuses on responding to the formal qualities of architecture when viewed from one static position. I am more interested in the aesthetic qualities of processes and relationships and the stories told about architecture when in motion. In researching this piece, I journeyed with Hawkins\Brown through their work, from the earliest projects in East London to ideas still nascent in the office.

connective aesthetics

Hawkins\Brown designed their first completed projects, Playbarn and PlayArc in 1989. Without three years of audited accounts, they were unable to be employed as architects by the London Borough of Newham. Instead, they created a design build company and sold their client a product. These projects are simple single storey barrel-vaulted structures, constructed of glulam portal frames and clad in aluminium. Although these buildings have a formal clarity, the simplicity of the gestalt object favoured by minimalist artists, they are at their best when considered as interactive places rather than static objects. Both suggested new ways of dealing with play in the local neighbourhood. The 'barns' do not only offer spaces for children to play, but they are pro-active, providing training for people working with children, toy libraries and workshops.

Art critic, Suzi Gablik, elaborating on her concept of "connective aesthetics", has argued for the importance of "listening" in the making of an artwork. For Gablik, listening rather than looking is what gives each person a voice, builds a community and makes art "socially responsive". She argues for "interactive and dialogic practices" that redefine the relationship of artist and spectator as connected rather than isolated. Gablik's conception of the self is 'field-like', where the individual artist is connected with the environment that they are situated within.

Gablik's critique of the autonomous artist resonates with the work of British Objects Relations theorists such as Donald Winnicott and Christopher Bollas around transitional objects and spaces. For Winnicott, the child's first 'not-me possession' occupies a transitional space between the inner imagination and the outer 'real' world. This transitional space is one of illusion, of play and also of aesthetic experience. Bollas later redefined this object and space as transformational, placing more emphasis on process rather than object, and on the mother's role in providing a holding environment that encouraged transformative processes to take place. For Bollas, the aesthetic moment is one linked to the memory of this transformative environment. Is it possible that certain kinds of architecture can occupy the place of the transitional object or the transformational environment and so play a similar role in inspiring play and change? If so, how much does this potential rely on the prior experience each individual brings to an environment and how much on the formal and spatial qualities of the architecture?

Certainly for Hawkins\Brown the process of designing a building is about responding to peoples' needs, however small and apparently insignificant. Playbarn is a self-contained structure in a park that is as low-key, yet striking, as the agricultural architecture it references. Despite being a strong sculptural form, it does not seek to make a clever architectural statement, but rather to "nurture and inspire" the community in Plaistow, East

London that it is part of. In this sense the architecture produces what Bollas would call a "holding environment" and in inspiring interaction and play it has the qualities of Winnicott's transitional space.

Russell Brown: It [Playbarn] has barely been cleaned in 13 years and the kids have scribbled their names on it. Some would say that's terrible, but it's not, it shows they love it.

Also located in East London, this time in East Ham, the Canteen was once a really un-welcoming pub, a strip joint, which was closed down by the police. As a result of their work on the Playbarns Hawkins\Brown got the job of refurbishing the building for a local community group, New Horizons, who had won awards for its work with nine to 14 year olds. Today New Horizons' New Canteen is the only place in the neighbourhood for teenagers where the 'no knives/no drugs' policy works.

The project was a refurbishment for what Hawkins\Brown admit to being a "stupidly low cost". Out of the £250,000 budget, £150,000 had to be spent on making the building structurally sound. Despite cost limitations, Hawkins\Brown managed to provide a whole series of new rooms for New Horizons: a multi-purpose space, fitness room and crèche downstairs, and a chill-out room, office and art-space upstairs. The internal finishes are by necessity extremely cheap: sterling board for the floors, shuttering ply for the walls and industrial light fittings. But the minimal gestures, generated out of economic pragmatism, produce a striking visual effect.

From the exterior the changes are slight but strategic. To the rear is a steel-fabricated balcony for smokers, and on the street façade a new glazed strip lit by a turquoise neon light has been set into a projecting zinc box. At the time Hawkins\Brown were interested in projects like the Dry Bar 201 by Ben Kelly Design in Manchester, which borrowed heavily from street signage and industrial architecture. This influence shows at the New Canteen, the architecture is an 'intervention', a new but bold layer added to an existing urban structure.

Jane Rendell: Given the difficulties of providing something of quality with such small budgets, are you still interested in seeking out projects like these?

RB: Well, we're more mindful now at the beginning, we don't promise the impossible so much.

David Bickle: But these projects are worthwhile. This architecture touches people in the way it should do. That's important to us, regardless of budget or brief.

JR: So what exactly counts as architecture for you? Could something as ordinary and small-scale as the insertion of a lift into a building be architecture?

RB: It can be if it transforms…

Roger Hawkins: If it makes something out of the work-a-day.

Hawkins\Brown's notion of the work-a-day can be related to Henri Lefebvre's concept of everyday life, a set of activities and practices that operate between domination and resistance, that speak of repetition and repression, but also offer 'moments' for transformation. Everyday architecture is usually considered to be low-key, almost invisible, not something developed through self-conscious designers. But often it is in projects with stringent economic limitations where new aesthetic languages are invented, where cheap and standard materials are used in new ways.

the power of place

For Hawkins\Brown, the cultural context of architecture is very important – "a building must respond to a specific context as well as have a life of its own", they say. It is important that the architecture is a response to the issues a specific site and group of people generate. In fine art, site-specific and context-based practice is assumed to be a critical activity, often based on a rejection of the traditional gallery system, but stemming from an interest in the languages and practices produced by particular places and people. In architecture, the term "site" tends to be understood as a static location rather than a set of relationships. Additionally, architecture that is "context specific" is often thought of in derogative terms, as conformist and unimaginative designs that go no further than copying the materials and formal features of their surroundings.

However, as Dolores Hayden discusses in The Power of Place, "the power of ordinary urban landscapes to nurture citizens' public memory, to encompass shared time in the form of shared territory", is key to the construction of local identity. Steve Pile and Michael Keith's edited collection of essays, Place and the Politics of Identity, also highlights the importance of identity to discussions of place. By interrogating the reciprocity of the relation between the politics of place and the place of politics these texts highlight an interest in places that are 'unfixed' and under construction. In developing the potential of relationships between the identities of different people and the places they inhabit, architecture has a vital role to play. Such work often involves dealing with the memories people have of a site and its history. Sometimes the architecture can work to retain certain historical moments or to recover past events, but at other times buildings are required to facilitate new attitudes to sites. The anthropologist Michel de Certeau, who defined space as a "practiced place" might call such architectural practices tactical in their desire to resist dominant readings of the site and produce new ones.

The Trowbridge Centre is a day centre for adults with learning difficulties designed by Hawkins\Brown in East London. The building has had a difficult emotional history, having been the scene of infamous cases of child abuse at the end of the 1970s. In the neighbourhood, the building had a poor reputation. The high wall surrounding it defined and heightened feelings of insularity, secrecy and fear. One of the first things that Hawkins\Brown did was to remove the wall and open up the building to the street. Today, the centre is surrounded by a leafy garden. From the street, through the vegetation, you can see into the main space, which appears very cosy, with golden coloured flooring and warm lighting. Once inside, despite the large expanse of glass, running floor to ceiling along the front façade, you don't feel exposed. Looking back out to the garden,

you feel protected, but not hemmed in.

Inside the building are a whole family of spaces offering varying levels of privacy and kinds of encounter. Key to the development of the programme has been the integration of different kinds of user, each with their own patterns of occupation. From the play buildings Hawkins\Brown learnt that office workers, by going in and out all the time, provide a continuous kind of use that maintains the building and keeps it feeling lived-in. This creates a helpful backdrop to the often more intermittent use of buildings by the 'community'. The demands on the Trowbridge Centre by different users have produced a layered design, in terms of its position on the site and the internal layout. There are places where local residents can bump into inhabitants, where office workers can encounter those using the day care centre, and spaces were people can simply be in a room on their own.

The architecture plays an important role in allowing this variation in meeting place. The building's response to the brief is more than passive backdrop, it actively creates an atmosphere, calm yet full of vitality. One of the most surprising moments in my time at the centre came when we were about to leave. Rather than one of the workers coming over to let us out, one of the day visitors opened the door for us, at the same time protecting another inhabitant who was threatening to wander out. This relaxed behaviour gave a clear indication of the degree of comfort and control very different inhabitants felt within the space.

JR: You've been working on this project for a long time, for six or seven years. It is architecture on a slow time-scale, a project that builds gradually.

RB: Yes, the Eames' do something they call "celebrating the building" where they are photographed on the structure as it is being constructed at every stage of the way. Early on at Trowbridge, we had an open day where we gave local residents seeds to plant and got a gardens project going. By coming in to do the gardening the local inhabitants became more comfortable with the place and came to learn that it was not actually dangerous. This means that once the buildings are finished, those who live around are already familiar with them.

JR: The work in the gardens, with the landscape designer, Jenny Coe, is very much about the process of making new relationships, connections with a site that help people identify with this place in a positive way.

RB: It is about making the connections first rather than getting on with the drawings, because if you get the connections right, then people bring the building with them.

the why and the how of the gift

The making and receiving of architecture could be considered an economy – a series of relationships of exchange between people. Buildings may be bought or sold like other exchangeable commodities, but what about the aspects of architecture, which are not exchanged for financial sums by individuals and corporations, but given as gifts? Many theorists resistant to the appropriating and accumulating tendencies of patriarchal capitalism have turned to alternative economies of exchange, such as gift giving, for inspiration. In gift giving, the economy of exchange is deferred; there is no knowing if and when a gift will be returned. There is also no knowing how a gift will be received. For French theorist, Hélene Cixous, the logic of the gift, "the why and the how of the gift", is one of generosity. This kind of logic can be found in Hawkins\Brown's aim to provide "buildings that not only realise the client's vision but transcend their original expectations".

Hawkins\Brown are currently working in Dalston, part of Hackney, again in East London, on a number of mixed-use schemes. The Gillett Square project is one that the office has been working on for five to six years. The site is on the west of Dalston High Street, a busy shopping street, with the culturally diverse Ridley Road market, on the opposite side of the street. Phase 1, the main building on Bradbury Street, containing 40 workshops, studios, shops and offices for artists, craftsmen, businesses and community groups, cost £240,000. Phase 2, costing £200,000, involved the design of ten market-stall units of 30m² each, with a shared store and toilets. These slick and robust 'pods' can be used as stalls, lock-ups and small walk-in shops and are rented out for £30 a week for starter businesses. When I visited all of the units were occupied, for example by a watch-repairers and a CD store. Roller shutters were open, music was playing loudly and stickers and signs had been pasted over the inclined fronts of the pods very definitely claiming the space as their own.

The client, Adam Hart, took a risk with this second phase of the project. Instead of turning their back on a parking lot, the market stalls face into it, creating the first stage in the transformation of this leftover space, towards becoming Gillett Square, a new urban square for Hackney. Hawkins\Brown have now got the job to redevelop the whole square and the building, Stamford Works, on the north side, and the Culture House, on the west side of the square. The idea is that the elevations of these buildings' will be completely clear, like a beacon shining out into the square.

RB: Again, it was an economy of means. We wanted to show change. We looked at training and management for what is a co-operative workspace and came up with the idea of open walkways, creating an urban theatre. This is still a hostile area and at the weekends it can feel unsafe. Having people looking out over the square has made it safer. And as soon as a couple of the market stalls were rented out it changed the nature of the place. The guys washing cars in the car park are great, because they police the square. But they also pop round and let people know if the busies are coming.

DB: The detail for the hatch of the market stalls was taken from car boots, making a sort of analogy between people buying goods and then opening up their car boots to put their shopping in. This is typical of some of our more recent work, where we are beginning to look outside of architecture for influence and inspiration, to popular culture, things that are actually quite immediate.

From anthropology, we have acquired 'material culture'; a phrase that refers to the cultural making and using of 'things' and allows us to view designed objects in relation to all kinds of other cultural artefacts. Andrew Cross is a photographer who has been interested in the mundane and banal architectures of the post-industrial global city for some years now. His interest is in the 'everyday', places involved in repetitive operations, dull and non-glamourous landscapes, around the edge of cities, often overlooked but central to the lives of many people: distribution centres, warehouses, suburban homes, petrol and service stations, out of town shopping centres. Cross is interested in the detail of such places, not in terms of the 'taste' and connoisseurship of high art and culture, but the differences in the lettering on delivery vans or the hedges of suburbia. One of his best-known works is a guidebook to the petrol stations of London.

As part of a project funded by the Royal Society of Arts' (RSA) Art for Architecture Award Scheme for collaborations between artists and architects, Cross has been working with Hawkins\Brown at Gillett Square. The Art for Architecture Award Scheme aims to challenge traditional modes of practice where artists are often asked to collaborate with architects at the last moment, when many of the key decisions of a design have already been made. In these instances an artist's skills are only employed in the decoration of a site or building, rather than something more strategic. By exchanging ideas at the earlier stages of a project, it is possible to reveal aspects of existing working procedures and forms of knowledge which are usually taken for granted. The RSA money is intended, then, to fund projects that enrich the working practices of both artists and architects. So far, working with Hawkins\Brown in Dalston, Cross has been using photography to uncover social processes. The intention is to produce a photo-essay (part of which is reproduced elsewhere in this book) that will record the transformation of this urban space.

DB: Andrew [Cross] is interested in infrastructure, but he is also interested in the relationships to spaces that are created as a result of infrastructure. What we want to do together has developed out of our earlier collaboration on the Hackney Town Square competition. Here Andrew was looking at the bus routes in and out of town, as a way of taking a message from Hackney out towards Trafalgar Square and the City of London. And we worked with the artist Bob and Roberta Smith, who came up with this slogan, "I believe in Hackney". What we would like to do here is propose a way in which the people of Hackney can understand the changes that are taking place as a result of the redevelopment of the square and think about how it relates to either their home or the city as a whole. So it is about looking in and looking out at the same time. Two ideas could become very much part of the architecture. One is a camera obscura, or some form of viewing device, so that people can gain an understanding of where the square sits in relationship to the city as a whole. The second is a way of elevating people so they can see where the town-square lies in relationship to where they live. So, the project is about helping people understand processes of urban change.

It is strange how often art and architecture are defined in relation to each other in a binary manner, where each is seen as something that the other is not. For example: art is for the individual/ architecture is social or architecture is functional/art has no function. I prefer to think of one in terms of the other. If we do this then art can be said to provide the place and occasion for certain modes of exchange 'to function' between people. Art can also be said to be 'useful' in providing certain kinds of moments, places and tools for self-reflection, critical thinking and radical practice. This seems to me to be the role that artist Cross has adopted within Hawkins\ Brown and particularly in his approach to the project in Dalston.

thinking is sculpting
Joseph Beuys' concept of social sculpture depends on the assumption that all human beings are artists, that they have the potential to image the world and also to re-imagine it. Beuys' thinking around

politics and pedagogic practice was greatly influenced by Fluxus, of whom he was a key member in the 1960s. Fluxus' work questioned the traditional separation made between art and life and the distinctions between artist and audience. Beuys is not suggesting that life is by definition already art or that life is already art. Rather that there is something particular to art – creative thinking and the use of the imagination – that can transform society and change the definitions and distinctions themselves. Rather than invite everyone to be an 'artist', Beuys called for creative thinking to enter all areas of life, including for example, law and science. "Thinking is sculpting", Beuys said.

The student union at Queen Mary and Westfield College in London was a £1.3 million project for Hawkins\Brown with some tight time constraints and a complex brief. Since the union had to function for the end of term ball and then re-open for freshers' week it had to be completed in only ten weeks. The existing building was not originally designed to cater for union functions and additionally it was being used for teaching. As well as adding new elements, a substantial reorganisation of the existing spaces was also required.

RH: The project was about extending the old building, connecting the new building back to the old building and re-establishing links within the old building. Most of it was internal reorganisation. I remember showing it to an architectural critic, who said, "What you've done here is like brain surgery; if a brain surgeon had made this series of complex interconnections and reconnections then it would be an amazing feat." But what we do can almost go unrecognised.

JR: Yes, although many people think of architecture as an art, they never locate the art of architecture in the creative act of solving problems, especially the sort that no one ever notices. A first time visitor, like me, is unable to take on board the kind of difficulties you had to sort out to simply make the building function in terms of level change for instance.

RH: One of the most rewarding experiences was being here when the second and third year students returned after being away for three months. They couldn't work out where they were, because the place had transformed so much. They stood at the front door with their jaws dropping.

Hawkins\Brown's restructuring of the Union building was the result of a highly pragmatic set of decisions made concerning the relationship between different parts of the building. How can the creativity required to solve such a complex set of problems be experienced and understood by the new user? Even if it could be, would it be thought of as 'art'? Is this the kind of thinking that Beuys might have called sculpting? For Beuys, an expanded notion of art includes the acts of thinking and speaking as valuable ways of shaping the world. On the one hand, his concept of 'plastik' thought and action requires a certain "coming to consciousness", on the other, social sculpture involves the ability to make invisible processes visible. Whether all kinds of architectural thought processes match up to Beuys' notion of social sculpture is debatable, but his ideas do allow us to consider the invisible discussions that take place in architectural design as part of the 'art' of architecture.

Some of the most creative work in architecture is carried out through professional and managerial decisions that structure the complex processes of consultation and collaboration with various clients and users. Not usually considered the 'art' of architecture, the design of such frameworks can be considered as valuable as any final object. The precise articulation and sensitive management of the relationship between architect, client and user requires careful deliberation. For Hawkins\Brown, these relationships constitute a major part of the conceptualisation and realisation of the projects, "working with users, funders, neighbours, consultants, contractors is critical to our ability to steer projects through briefing, planning, design and construction". The Tottenham Court Road project in Central London, the design of a major new transport interchange, is really putting this belief to the test. The new site will have to deal with the passage of 120,000 people per day. As the lead consultants, Hawkins\Brown has taken on board the views and advice of over 100 representations from consultants, clients and local government.

RH: We got involved in Tottenham Court Road Underground Station through Crossrail whose policy was to employ younger firms of architects to help dress out some of the larger civil-engineered spaces. We've actually stayed with it through four or five different clients. Because Crossrail was on hold, we found ourselves working for the Northern Line Project team, then the Jubilee, Northern Line and Piccadilly Infrastructure Company and now Tubelines. So it is complicated politically. Frankly it's to do with where the money comes from. We are talking about a £75 million public investment, where not one institution necessarily wants to foot the bill. So there is a lot of behind the scenes politics in how things get rationalised.

JR: There seems to be a big question about where the edge of the public realm is located – is it along the line of ticket gates or where the scheme hits the surface?

RH: The operational railways are primarily concerned about the station but everyone recognises that the Ticket Hall roof will form a fantastic new public space around Centre Point. Our role is to provide the design vision for this new urban square. It is anticipated that developers of adjacent sites will have to put money into public space; our role is to avoid a patchwork. At Trowbridge for example, where we had a client with no money, we had to operate politically to get 'architecture'. Here we also have to be astute as to how things operate.

the guarantor of two intentionalities

The French philosopher, Luce Irigaray has written much on the politics of relationships. In reconfiguring the phrase "I love you" as "I love to you", she argues for the importance of the word "to" as a sign of mediation between two people. The "to" for Irigaray avoids reducing a person to an object, and guarantees two 'intentionalities'. This reconfiguration of language allows us to think about how relationships are constructed between two subjects, rather than between objects and subjects. In turn this provides a way of rethinking the kind of personal relations and intentions involved in architecture in terms of reciprocity, rather than possession, ownership or annihilation.

Related to the idea of reciprocity, is Irigaray's understanding of "caress", a gesture that "unfolds as an intersubjective act, as a communication between two". Irigaray's "caress" is a "gesture-word" that describes an interaction between two people rather than the imposition of one on another. This provides an interesting way of considering the 'intention' of the architect and the notion of 'concept' in architectural design. Instead of generating abstract formal concepts that get applied later on, Hawkins\Brown's projects suggest that it is possible to generate a design out of a relationship with the site or the brief. These ways of working are often more evident in the early stages of project design rather than the finished building.

One of Hawkins\Brown's new projects is for a Maggie's Cancer Care Centre in Sheffield. The centre aims to provide non-institutional care for people diagnosed with cancer and their carers, families and friends. It is part of a larger programme of further buildings for cancer care being developed by architects such as Zaha Hadid, Daniel Libeskind and Frank Gehry. Hawkins\Brown explained to me that when Maggie Jencks was diagnosed with cancer it was in a hospital corridor with fluorescent lights. The environment was very impersonal and in her writings she expressed a need for 'domesticity' during her illness, for a place that was much more homely. The site for Hawkins\Brown's building is an Edwardian villa built of sandstone, located near to the Royal Hallamshire Hospital in Sheffield, with views out to the surrounding hills.

DB: In our proposal for the Maggie's Centre, we choose some evocative images of home. One of them was of Vita Sackfield West's library at Sissinghurst. It is an image of just one room, but it contained everything we thought our client wanted in the building. We presented images superimposed with words, so that people could read the two together. I think this fired up the clients because we didn't show them an object or a thing, no super-gesture.

JR: This super-gesture is what a lot of architects call concept, but it is often nothing more than an unusual form and rarely contains an idea that is social or critical.

DB: Yes, and then the programme is punched into that formal gesture. I think our approach is very different and just as important to this particular project. At the Maggie's Centre we looked initially at presenting something that didn't commit, yet was rich enough to take forward certain aspects of the brief.

In the case of the Maggie's Centre, Hawkins\Brown's initial response to certain emotional qualities of space suggested in the brief has been to use image and text to evoke a sense of the place they hope to create. Working with the juxtaposition of image and text allows the viewer to perceive a 'third space' that is not determined by the word or the image but suggested by the space between the two.

In another project also nascent in the office, the Roald Dahl Museum and Children's Literature Centre, the site has been the most important starting point. The site, acquired by Lizzy Dahl, is a collection of ramshackle buildings, formally a coaching inn, in Great Missenden. The new building will include galleries, an archive, a studio for a writer in residence, a shop, offices and an interactive studio. Since some of the buildings have appeared in Quentin Blake's illustrations of Dahl's stories, they are already part of Dahl culture. This has presented a particular kind of problem to Hawkins\Brown:

DB: The site is quite a challenge. Because a lot of the material is already there, we've got to tease the project out of the site.

RH: I think our intervention on the Roald Dahl project will have quite a light touch and deliberately so. There are parallels back to the New Canteen where we also had a light touch, but that was forced onto us by a complete lack of budget. Here we will have a light touch that comes as a response to the buildings we are working with.

DB: It is quite interesting for us to explore things in different ways. Small projects allow us to look at a conceptual approach to projects. They provide a seed bed for other ideas, bigger ones.

JR: How do you think you can bring conceptual thinking to bear on complex social projects?

RH: The planning process has forced a lot of developers to think about mixed-use schemes on tight urban sites, shared ownership of housing, a complete mix of people living together, with bars, cafes, cultural and leisure activities. This sort of mixed-use work is very interesting to us, because it allows us to do on one site what we have previously been doing on lots of different sites.

JR: Are you thinking about mixed-use in a brand new way, or are there particular precedents that you are trying to develop and evolve?

RH: Our work is about what I would call "an approach to architecture". The 'swirl of the cape' architecture produces an image and that's it. An image is enough to produce an office block – which is fairly straightforward. But our background, around existing buildings, is about working with the complexities of briefs and bringing different constraints and opportunities to bear on a problem. An image doesn't produce that kind of architecture.

Hawkins\Brown have also been working on a private house for the artist, Rachel Whiteread, which has just been completed in East London. For almost a decade, from her first public work, House, 1993, the cast of a Victorian terraced house in East London, to her more recent intervention, an inversion set on top of the empty plinth in Trafalgar Square, Whiteread has been working with notions of absence. In plaster and resin, she takes hollows, gaps and cavities, sometimes of existing structures, other times of imagined spaces, and makes emptiness manifest.

For example, Whiteread's Holocaust Memorial, Jüdenplatz Vienna, 1995, is a concrete cast of a library, with double doors, a ceiling rose and lined with thousands of books, that sits at the northern end of the square on the excavations of a thirteenth century synagogue. The site has a turbulent history, in the fifteenth century Jews committed mass suicide by going down into the crypt and burning themselves alive.

Like most public monuments Whiteread's memorial is a solid and visible historical marker, but its quiet presence does not attempt to confirm the facts, rather it makes their absence tangible. Her rewriting of history is not the insertion of more text, but a marking of the places that history has never allowed to exist: the gaps between the lines, the silences between the words, the stories that get left untold.

Whiteread is a private person and so her house designed by Hawkins\Brown has not received any publicity. But given that the artist demonstrates a particular characteristic to her work – a tactic of making absence present – many have wondered whether she would take her ways of making art into the design of her home. It turns out that this is the case, but in a subtle and unexpected way. Her house is not a cast, nor does it contain the casts of any objects or spaces; the connection with her artwork is more tangential. Her new home is located in a 1958 synagogue in East London. The former religious hall is now her studio and archive. Whiteread has chosen to situate her work in a space with a powerful history. Is this a place where the past has been emptied out? or where the memories of that past are still present in traces? Hawkins\Brown's work has been characteristically low-key. Two new rooftop pavilions housing an apartment and a library are lightweight structures built from cement fibre cladding systems. There is no 'super-gesture' here, rather in Irigaray's terms, this architecture is evidence of two intentionalities, a 'gesture-word' that gives space for the artist's and architect's intentions to co-exist.

There was a period in the 1990s, when the architectural avant-garde assumed that social architecture was unlikely to produce inspiring buildings, presumably as a response to the lack of aesthetic innovation of much of the 'community architecture' of the 1980s. Will Alsop's Peckham Library, the building that won the Stirling Prize for Architecture in 2000, seems to have changed all of that. Community architecture is fashionable again. So does this mean that we can have ethics and aesthetics rather than choose between the two? I hope so, for this would make space in current architectural debate for Hawkins\Brown. Rather than locate aesthetics solely in the field of the visual, Hawkins\Brown practice architecture in a way that rethinks aesthetics in terms of ethics, and take architecture as a social process as well as a product. Hawkins\Brown's architecture demands to be understood less as a collection of objects and more as collection of social processes – as the traces of the relationships people make with one another.

THIS IS NOT AN ENGINEER WRITING IT, SO DO NOT BE AN ENGINEER SEEING IT.

THE WORLD IS ONE BIG HOUSING ESTATE AND NO-ONE'S COLLECTING THE RUBBISH.

So what do you reckon to this?
Text and photographs by Andrew Cross

Canning Town, East London, in February, in the pouring rain. It does not feel like the prettiest of places, at least not today. Evidence of a challenging urban environment: physical decay, poverty, struggling public services, some people in difficult circumstances. Most of all it is wet and grim. You squint with your eye and try and imagine this as a happier place, but it is not easy. However, regeneration is approaching on the horizon: new roads, new buildings, and the channel tunnel raillink in neighbouring Stratford.

What do we ask of architecture in such situations? More than anything perhaps somewhere warm and dry. Also, I want the new building sites to be interesting. Some mess, of course, but a few clues each day to indicate what is happening. Some things that may provide some belief in the future.

New buildings can be exciting but the destruction of others and the clearing of space can be more refreshing. Once completed it is often necessary to move onto the next thing.

I get in my car to drive to the next place, but mostly to get out of the rain. From a car architecture is glanced, as it

is from the bus or even when walking along the pavement. It is caught in the corner of our eye: peeping over a wall, appearing around the corner or stuck behind a lorry. Even the building that is my next destination is at its most memorable as I first see it when turning a corner. What role does design, function, engineering and detail play in this experience? I really don't know.

Is there a theory for all this? Something that either determines how we arrive at this situation or explains how we got there after the event? Probably, but I don't know it. I doubt also whether theories make that much difference on a miserable day.

The most we can ask of architecture is that we might notice it. Architecture that is okay to glance. At the very least, we should expect architecture that does a job. Like provide decent shelter from the weather and grime. Somewhere where people might gather. Somewhere children can play without people worrying if the kids will make a mess.

& SPECIALITY GASES

STARE AT A WHITE WALL EVERY 15 PAGES.

THINK OF YOURSELF AS THE FREEHOLDER.

2
people

Women's Pioneer Housing Association Headquarters London

Bridging over a familiar headquarters
building to offer a whole new lease of life
for the housing association.

people are the most interesting thing[1];
not buildings;
why talk concrete when there's flesh;
people are amazing;
that's why we get up in the morning;
to meet people;
building is a social process;
like Joseph Beuys' social sculpture;
everything's social deep down;
hello;
we all have to relate;
we're human beings;
a social species;
buildings are the result;
of a series of relationships[2];
created between people;

[1]Women's Pioneer Housing Association Headquarters;
 Built another floor on top;
 Moved 35 staff upstairs without stopping work;

[2]Woodley Town Council hired Arts consultant Brian Harris;
 Brian Harris called Hawkins\Brown;
 Hawkins\Brown showed Henry Moore Foundation;
 The Oakwood Centre happened;
 Theatre, café, community hall, town council forum and garden
 by flower terrorist Jinny Blom;

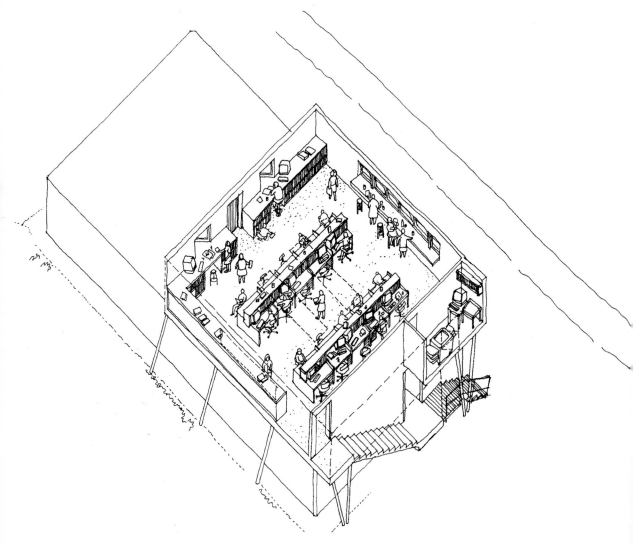

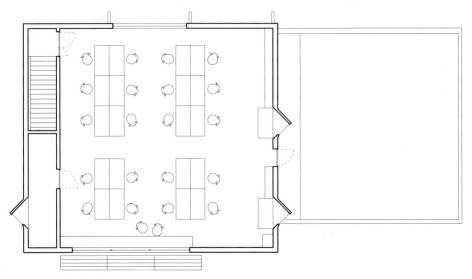

First Floor Plan

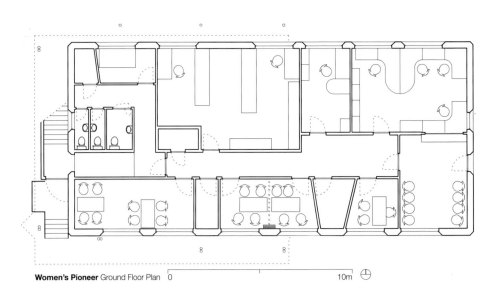

Women's Pioneer Ground Floor Plan　　0　　　　　　　　　　10m

nurture;
why so alien to architects;
too many men;
we must nurture;
to inspire;
collaborate with artists and folk;
create extra engagement;
beyond the building itself;
get nurturing;

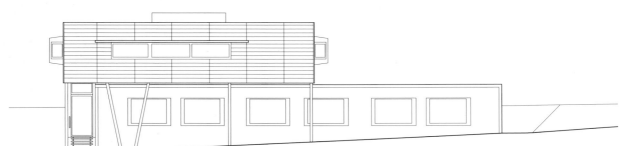

South Elevation

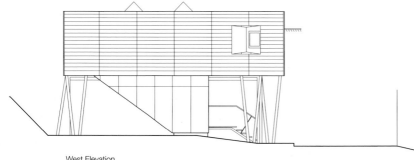

West Elevation

READ THE FOLLOWING SENTENCE OUT LOUD: BUILDINGS SHOULD NURTURE AND INSPIRE.

The Oakwood Centre
Woodley

Unique funding approach to collect
together a new theatre, community hall,
café and forum for the town council.

we practice unbuilding;
use up the bad bits of a site first;
save the good bits;
canny economy;
the knack of change;
change little yet affect much;
spend where you need change;

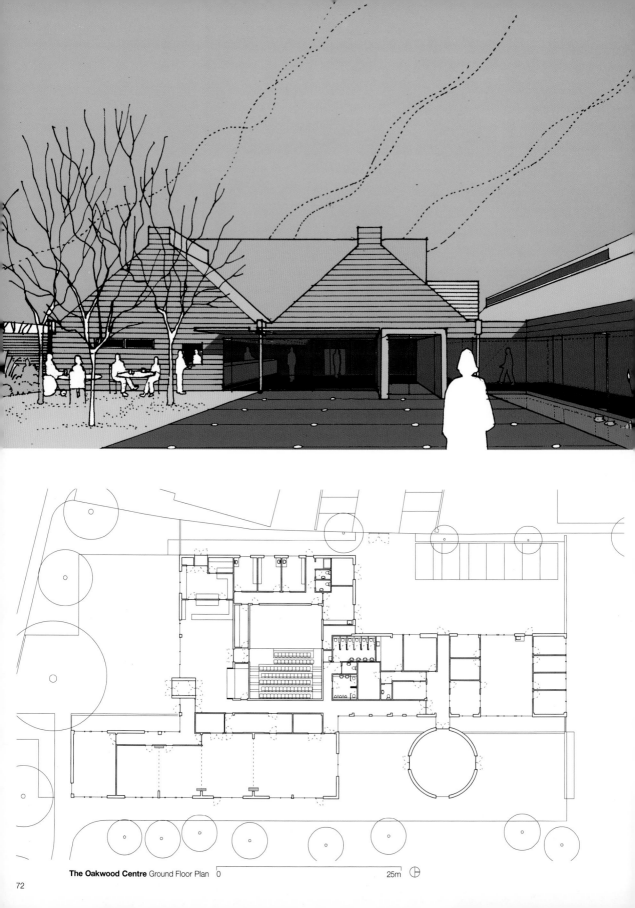

The Oakwood Centre Ground Floor Plan   0   25m

Elevation

Section

Stamford Works
/Gillett Place
London

New thinking about living in the city,
about buying art – new ways of
inclusive and creative consultation
as part of the process.

relationships are everything;
they build the buildings;
old buildings for sure;
clients tell all;
how noisy it is;
where and when the sun hits;
crawl around, get filthy;
but dialogue goes deeper;
between cavity walls;
of new and old brick;
from nature to man-made;
subtle discussions[1];
never-ending;

[1]Stamford Works;
Unique partnership of public, private and voluntary sectors;
Spawned Hackney Culture House, Gillett Square,
Bradbury St Workshops;
£9.6 million on local life;

Stamford Works phase 1
Client
Macdonald Egan
Description
Mixed use commercial:
7 private residential units
11 affordable residential units
8 BI/C3 units
Design
July 2002

Community Workshops, Bradbury St
Client
Hackney Co-operative Developments
Description
Refurbishment of terrace for community managed BI workspaces
Design
Sept 1995 – June 1996

Stamford Works phase 2
Client
Macdonald Egan
Description
Mixed use commercial:
36 private residential units
3 live/work units
Design
July 2002 – 2003

Market Stalls, Bradbury St
Client
Hackney Co-operative Developments
Description
Community managed retail units (market stalls)
Café and amenity area fit out
Design
November 1997 – May 1999

Stamford Works phase 3
Client
Macdonald Egan
Description
Mixed use commercial:
3 retail units
18 live/work units
Design
January 2002 – 2005

Culture House Bradbury St
Client
Hackney Co-operative Developments
Description
Community forum
Design
July 2001 – 2004

Gillett Square
Client
Gillett Square Partnership:
London Borough of Hackney
Hackney Co-operative Developments
Groundworks Hackney
Macdonald Egan
Greater London Authority
Description
Public/private funded square
Design
January 2001 – 2005

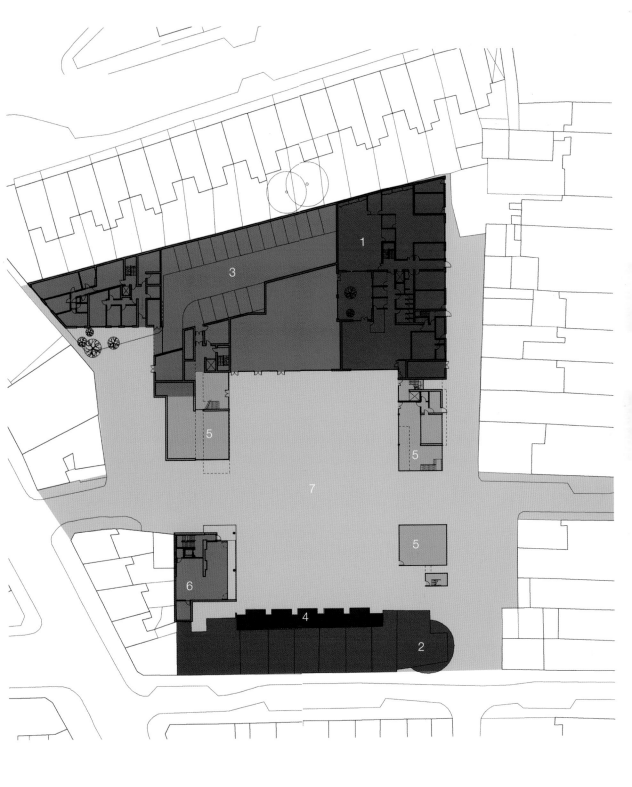

Market Stalls
Bradbury St
London

Dubbed an 'urban souk' by Wallpaper* –
prefabricated market units – a truly
multi-cultural piece of urban design.

From cardboard
model to shining
steel materiality –
realising the market
stalls; Dalston

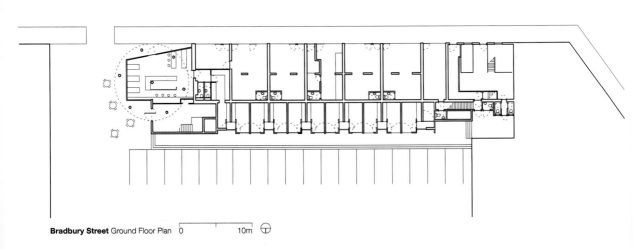

Bradbury Street Ground Floor Plan 0   10m

Elevation

PRESS FLOWERS FROM EACH SITE IN THE APPROPRIATE PAGES.

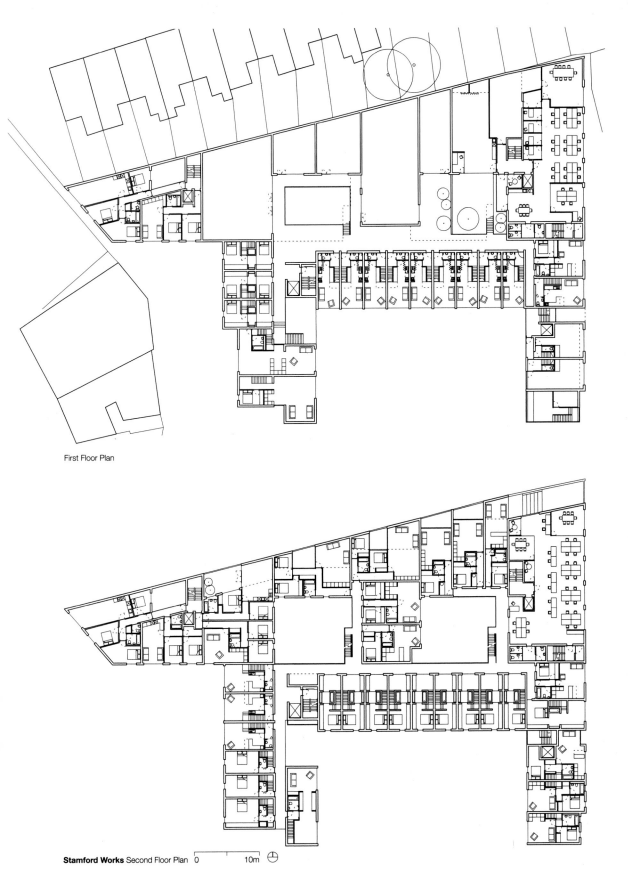

First Floor Plan

Stamford Works Second Floor Plan   0   10m

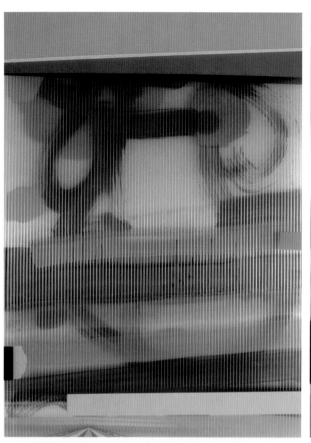
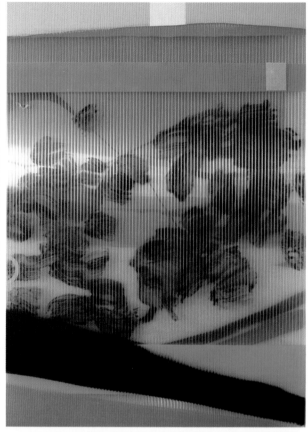

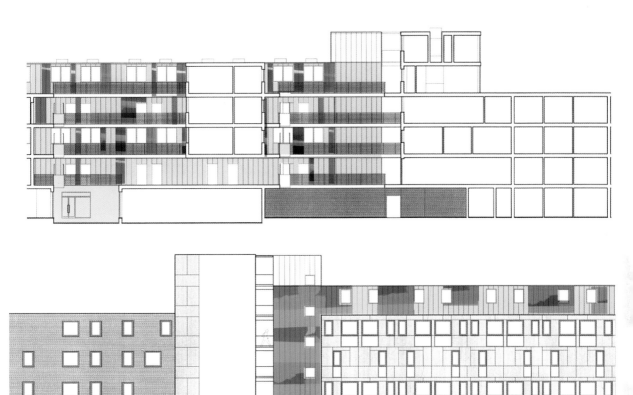

Danny Rolph's large
scale paintings on
polycarbonate that
will form the four
storey elevation
to Gillett Square

things happen in circles;
pull out all the stops and goodness loops;
comes back to you;
and some;
complimentary Chinese whispers[1];
snowballing;
all people want;
is to work with people they like;
people who are good at what they do;
look for these patterns;
they come in circles[2];

[1]Adam Hart of Hackney Co-operative Developments;
6 years whispering;
Created Bradbury Street Community Workshops;
Voted best new retail space in Europe by Design Week in 2001;

[2]Squares too;
A new town square called Gillett;
Best 100 new spaces for London;

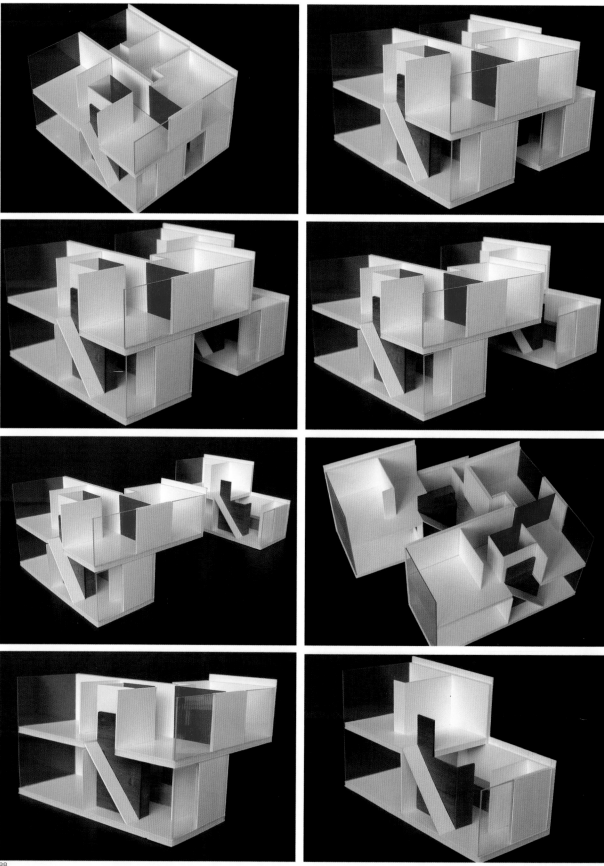

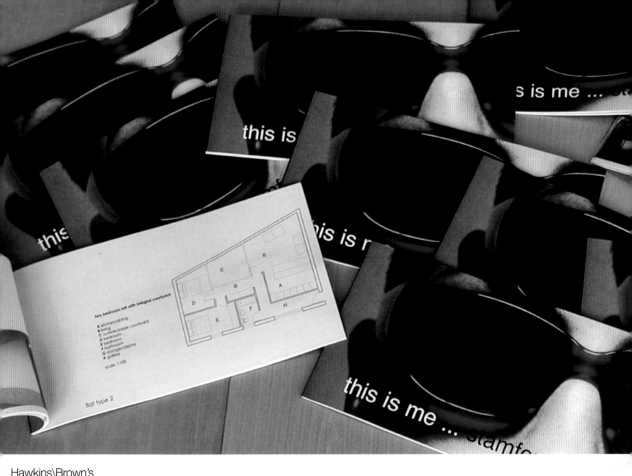

Hawkins\Brown's
marketing material
for Stamford Works

locals know best;
better than a blueprint;
how to renew;
the desperate and desolate;
how the deeply deprived excites us[1];
so involve them;
let locals drive design;
lead us;
from trespassers to strangers;
to visitors to residents;
a one eighty;
on how to think;

[1]Rundown car park became beacon of business and art;
The Culture House, Hackney;

house

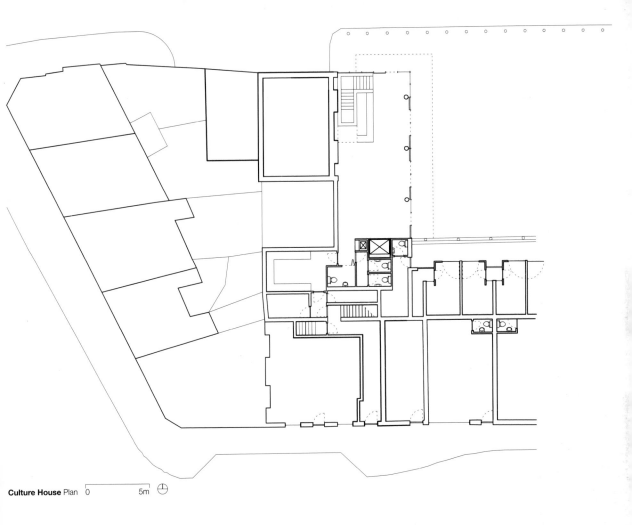

Culture House Plan 0   5m

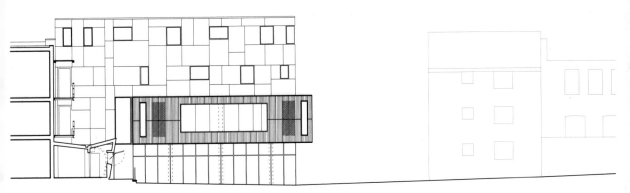

Elevation

3
openness

PlayArc and Playbarn, Newham

Sold as a product including buildings, furniture and equipment – a cutting edge response to the need for playbuildings.

must remain lucid;
fixed views encumber progress;
opinions are like buildings;
some movement is healthy;
have a sense of it;
trust instinct;
what starts out as one thing;
may become two things;
the more rigid we are;
the more tense we are;
the more fragile we are;

PlayArc and Playbarn, Newham;
Invented modular system;
Evolved for Stratford training centre;
Refined for Leyton;

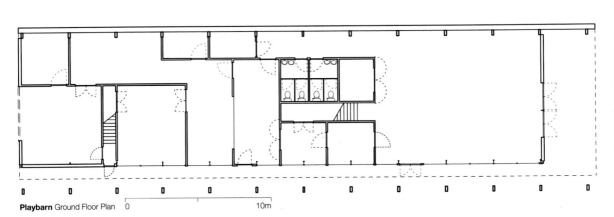

Playbarn Ground Floor Plan   0   10m

Section

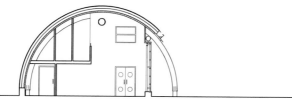

Elevation

LICK YOUR FINGERS LIKE BANK TELLERS TO TURN PAGES.

REINCARNATE YOURSELF AS A BIRD AND LAND ON EACH ROOF.

3 Mills
Play and Training Centre

Development of the Playbarn adding
teaching and conference space.

The collaboration between architecture and social action
Mark Harrison and Dave Ward

Over the last 17 years Hawkins\Brown and the Centre for Social Action (CSA) have collaborated on a range of projects forging a unique partnership between community development and architecture through a series of often difficult regeneration projects – true 'action research'. The two organisations also work together on Hawkins\Brown projects that require initiating development or have real opportunities for the involvement of the community in the design process. There is a great deal of synergy in this working relationship, bringing together meaningful community engagement with reliable architectural support.

This partnership, between community development and architecture addresses, from different professional perspectives, a critical understanding of urban design. It provides a model for creating new environments, both virtual and actual, that have a positive impact on the lives of communities. Our partnership is in contrast to many approaches that are strong on rhetoric and publicity but weak on theory and method. The root causes of the failure of large scale urban regeneration is largely one of "more of the same" – new words, same old methods.

The collaboration began in 1986/1987 and predates the formation of Hawkins\ +Brown. Mark Harrison was employed by the Homeless Network in London to develop a Day Centre for Homeless Young People in the West End as part of the International Year of the Homeless. The work was overseen by a multi-agency steering group, that included architects. Best practice suggested that homeless young people should be involved in the design and development process. This concept was greeted with scepticism and doubt by most of the youth workers involved but enthusiastically embraced by Russell Brown, who was the young project architect given the job to sort out the details.

It was Hawkins\Brown's optimism and professional acceptance that it is the most obvious thing in the world to consult the end users of a building about its design that forged the professional relationship. The acceptance of homeless young people as 'clients' to take a brief from was inspiring and demonstrated a commitment to equality that the youth workers could have learnt from. What followed was a genuinely creative process where we all learnt a lot and the young people involved got a youth centre they were proud of.

Another lesson learnt at the Day Centre was that the initial consultation established an unquestionable need for this facility in the West End so that at each stage – when the project was challenged at funding, planning or seeking institutional support – the need for the project had been independently established.

From this start a community business and research group has developed around the principle of social action to create the Centre for Social Action, a research, training, consultancy unit based at De Montford University, Leicester. Social Action is an approach to practice, training and research which starts from the issues, ideas and understanding of community members, rather than from a professional's definition of their needs. A central tenet is respect for and a positive view of communities, particularly the poor and marginalised in society. Social Action emphasises that a key responsibility of practitioners, academics and researchers is to facilitate a process of learning, development and change. This involves specific skills and knowledge which are not the province of any one group or profession, but should be available and accessible to all.

Other joint projects between CSA and Hawkins\Brown included Four Walls – Housing Homeless People, a three way project between Hawkins\Brown, the Centre for Social Action and The Homeless Services Agency. The project set out to identify, survey and make proposals for empty and disused buildings in London so as to bring them back into use for homeless people. The partnership was engaged by the Tree of Life Trust, the managers of Tent City, which provides cheap accommodation for young people visiting London. Their vision was to create a permanent youth exchange centre, using their base on Wormwood Scrubs. This project involved combining a youth centre with environmentally friendly and community sensitive buildings.

In 1999 Hawkins\Brown introduced the Centre for Social Action to a commercial developer, Macniven and Cameron, who needed to identify a 'planning benefit' package to unlock a potential site for a multiplex cinema. CSA carried out consultations with the local community which identified a number of unforeseen views. Firstly, the local people were keen to see a multiplex cinema as a leisure facility in an isolated estate in Ramsgate. In addition they saw the cinema complex as offering jobs and attracting public transport connections. All this was in direct opposition to the town centre based planning policy of the local authority. The commercial developer could see the value of 'real' rather than tokenistic consultation because it gave them a strong basis on which to argue the case for their development and a better understanding of their own local audience.

The CSA has been involved in Hawkins\Brown projects for New Horizons (a youth club in Stratford, East London), Hackney Community College, Barnet Voluntary Services Council and a group from the Notting Hill Carnival who wanted to establish a permanent museum and workshop for the design and construction of the carnival costumes.

There are a number of features of all this early work that were seen as innovative in the mid 1980s and are still so today. These features help define and are defined by a process of social action:

Redefining Professional Roles
The partnership changed the relationship between the professional architect or community development worker and the end users/community members.

The joint approach views people as stakeholders and experts about their lives, with knowledge and experience that can enhance and improve the design process. A relationship that is forged in respect for each others life skills, experiences and knowledge is the starting point for a dynamic and creative process which,

in turn, leads to better architecture and design.

Citizen Engagement
The partnership view people as active citizens, equals and experts in their own world. They initiated open and transparent processes that respect individual and community views, using methods that people can engage with in an active and meaningful way. The professionals need to demonstrate respect for each others skills through partnership.

Sustainable
Community involvement at each stage of the process in a meaningful way helped achieve end user satisfaction and ownership of finished product.

The skill for the trained professionals, whatever their roles, is in enabling community development to take place through a transparent and negotiated process. The professionals need to focus on enabling community members through involvement and engagement thereby creating ownership and sustainability after involvement has ended.

Optimism
Professionals have a responsibility to be optimistic, positive and believe that positive social change is achievable through working in partnership.

Commercial Attitude
In Ramsgate the CSA worked for a commercial developer and carried out a community consultation to establish views on the development potential for a site adjacent to a socially excluded area. The work established community views on the potential leisure development and multiplex site.

Swimming Against the Tide
In 2001 the partnership conducted a community consultation for New Deal for Communities, West Ham and Plaistow, in the Eastlea area, around the proposed development of a community resource centre. The consultation revealed deep scepticism in the local community. The

expressed needs of the community did not fit with the views of New Deal representatives or officers, so there was tension between commissioners and the team over the outcomes. The final report included service and facility recommendations alongside building plans.

Addressing Social Exclusion

In launching the Social Exclusion Unit in 1997, Tony Blair pointed out that: "Social Exclusion is about income, but it is also about more. It is about prospects, networks and life chances."

The government has targeted truancy and school exclusion, street living and the problems of crime, drugs, unemployment, community breakdown, poor health, and low educational achievement as critical problems that blight certain areas of our country. These are indeed potent symbols of social exclusion. How we deal with these is key to the success of physical and social regeneration.

The government has put in place a panoply of schemes to tackle these problems: Sure Start, Education Action Zones, Health Action Zones, New Deal for Communities, to name only some. Potentially they have real substance and a commitment of both resources and political will to sustain them, but the question is not simply what is on offer but how it is offered.

We live in a climate in which the rhetoric of involvement and participation is everywhere. But is it worth more than the paper it is written on? Participation is too often reduced to after-the-event complaints procedures, impersonal surveys or superficial unfocussed 'consultations'. By intent, or more often, by default, the agenda remains in the control of the provider.

"Participation by invitation" does not work. It may even engender a reaction against professionals who impose agendas, whether in a superficially participative way or not. Indeed, this can add to a sense of alienation, pushing people further away, towards rejecting a society which they probably see as having failed and rejected them anyway. There is no use in professional workers and policy makers continuing to

set the agenda. If they do so, they will fail to offer people anything with which to engage. It may even force them further outside, reinforcing alienation and exclusion.

Instead, what we seek to create is a genuine exchange in a climate of open partnership between user and provider. For this it is essential that:
– Intention and process are made explicit.
– People engage in discussion and reflection. This enables them to gain understanding and a real sense of ownership of what is involved.
– Then, on this basis, people are able to give an aware and informed consent to contributing their time and energy.

This is inclusive participation. It involves:
– Bringing people to meaningful decisions.
– Offering real choices.
– Sharing information.
– Sharing responsibility.
– Openness and clarity about scope, but also about boundaries: specifying what are the workers' responsibilities and the expectations they carry from their managers and political masters. What is the power they will and must hold regardless?

Being Part of the Solution Not Part of the Problem

What does this mean in practice? CSA and Hawkins\Brown have tried to apply these principles in addressing the Government's Social Exclusion and Regeneration agenda. Our approach is based on a critical perspective of conventional approaches.

The economic and social benefits of regeneration need to stay local. It means that investment in communities must benefit communities. So often the main beneficiaries of programmes live and work outside the areas in whose name the regeneration scheme is happening. This means building the social capital and capacity in communities to fully participate and engage in the development and regeneration process. It means using resources in a different way. It requires a critical re-evaluation of the role professionals play. The joint approach is to work in partnership, alongside people and communities. Professionals need to be 'on tap' not 'on top'. The skill for the trained professional, whatever their role, is in enabling the community development to take place through a transparent and negotiated process. To resource the community for planning and change – involvement, engagement and ownership are the cornerstones of our approach.

The Role of Social Action
The main feature of Social Action – which distinguishes it from other approaches – is that it recasts the role of the professional worker. It intentionally strives to integrate into the practice the criticisms of professionals that have come from service users and communities. The challenge is to make sense of the role of the professional and transform it from being part of the problem to being part of the solution. What has emerged is a way of working that redefines this role, be it practitioner, manager, trainer or researcher. The worker does not lead but through a highly skilled process, facilitating service users and community members in making choices and taking action themselves.

From the work of the Centre for Social Action we conclude that, to put it plainly, it means asking the question why? This is not simply a mechanical exercise. Asking 'why?' links action with the exploration of root causes. This twin track process is essential if people are to gain real and sustainable control over their situations.

In professional practice, as in real life, we too readily leap from what questions (what is wrong?) to how questions (what can we do about it? how should we proceed?). In doing this we unwittingly steer explanations, responsibilities and the scope of solutions to the private world around people, keeping understanding and action within their existing knowledge and experience. This knowledge and experience has been fashioned by people's positions in society. For the excluded, this means the exclusionary processes which keep them there.

In asking 'why?' people can pursue an issue until the root causes have been identified and exposed. Asking why gives people the opportunity to break out of the demoralising and self-perpetuating narrowness of vision and self-blame which has been created by poverty, lack of opportunity and exclusion. When horizons of what is possible expand, people come up with new explanations for problems and ideas for tackling them. By asking the question why we can turn the spotlight away from people as problems, to the problems they face, and enable them to envision a much wider range of options for action and change.

Opportunity
The government, by providing both resources and institutional frameworks, is seeking to regenerate communities and connect the excluded to the pathways of opportunity. Without question, these are laudable objectives. However, these initiatives are strong on objectives and frameworks, on the 'what', but they give little attention to 'how', to the process of engaging the intended beneficiaries through inclusive participation and, hence, asking the essential, but radical, question, 'why?'

The partnership has demonstrated and refined a methodology that strives to create better design and environments for people and communities so that physical regeneration is in line with the aspirations and needs of the people who have to live, work and use the spaces and buildings created. We also believe that regeneration can only be effective when approached holistically, involving the community and end users from the outset and throughout the process.

WHAT COLOUR ARE THE WORDS HACKNEY TOWN HALL SQUARE?

Tottenham Court Road Station London

An integrated transport interchange – linking a new ticket hall for the Tube and CrossRail with a major public space in front of CentrePoint.

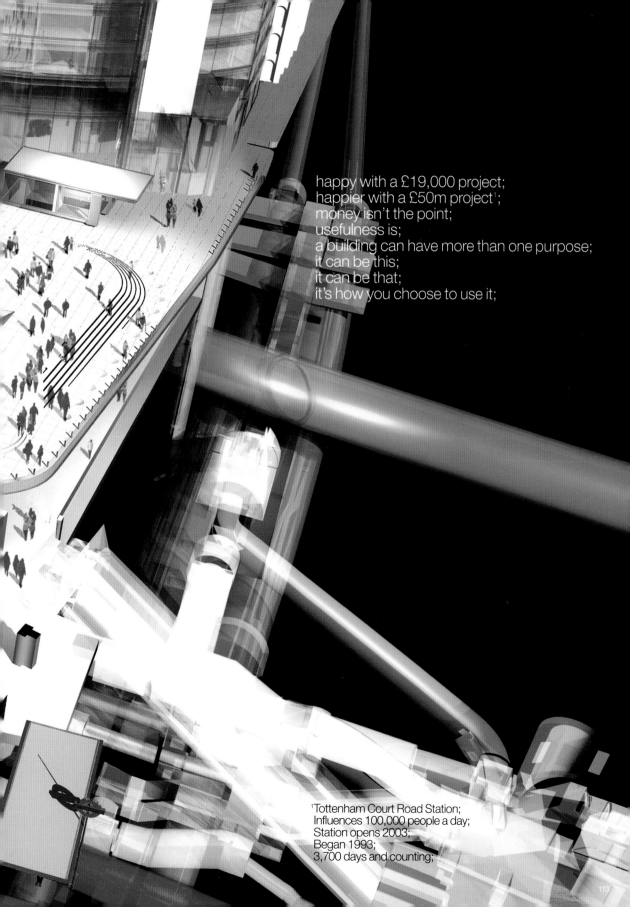

happy with a £19,000 project;
happier with a £50m project[1];
money isn't the point;
usefulness is;
a building can have more than one purpose;
it can be this;
it can be that;
it's how you choose to use it;

[1]Tottenham Court Road Station;
Influences 100,000 people a day;
Station opens 2003;
Began 1993;
3,700 days and counting;

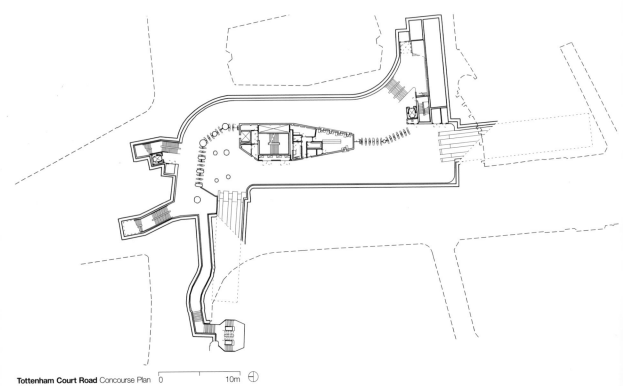

Tottenham Court Road Concourse Plan   0   10m

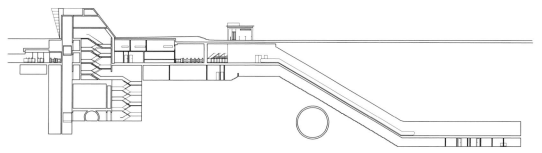

Section

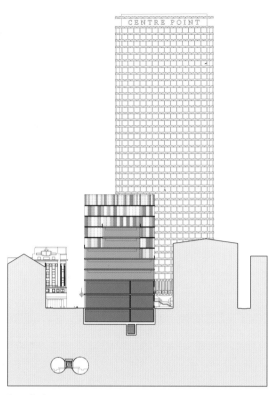

Cross Section

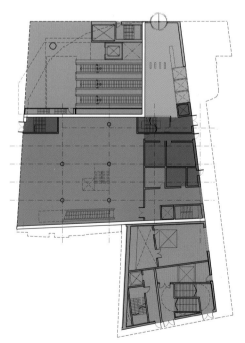

Ground Floor Plan

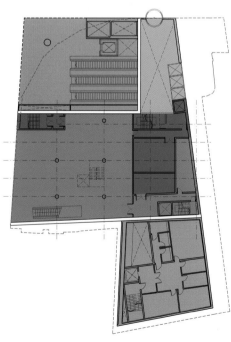

First Floor Plan

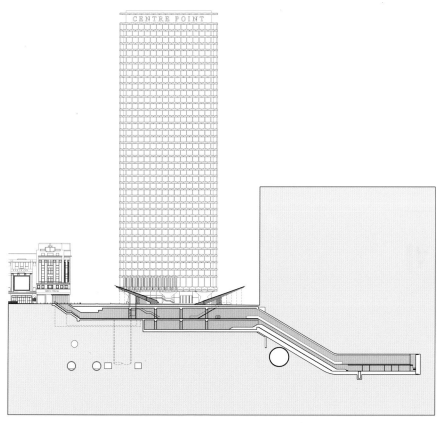

Cross Section Through Station

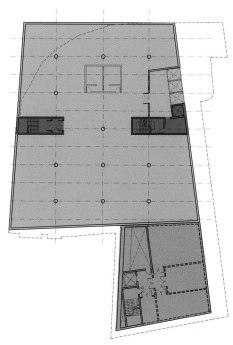

Second Floor Plan

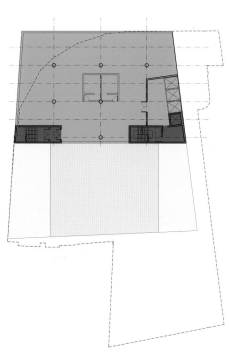

Typical Upper Floor Plan

projects never end:
only boredom seeks an end;
also is cul-de-sac-less;
no end is dead;
buildings must live;
for the people inside them;
to make them feel alive;
even if they're dead;
like in crematoriums;
we should never exclude;
explain it to a child;
or the world's most famous designer[1];
the same story;
the story of also;

[1]The man who invented that lemon squeezer;
In current project with Hawkins\Brown;

DRAW A MAP OF IT FROM MEMORY.

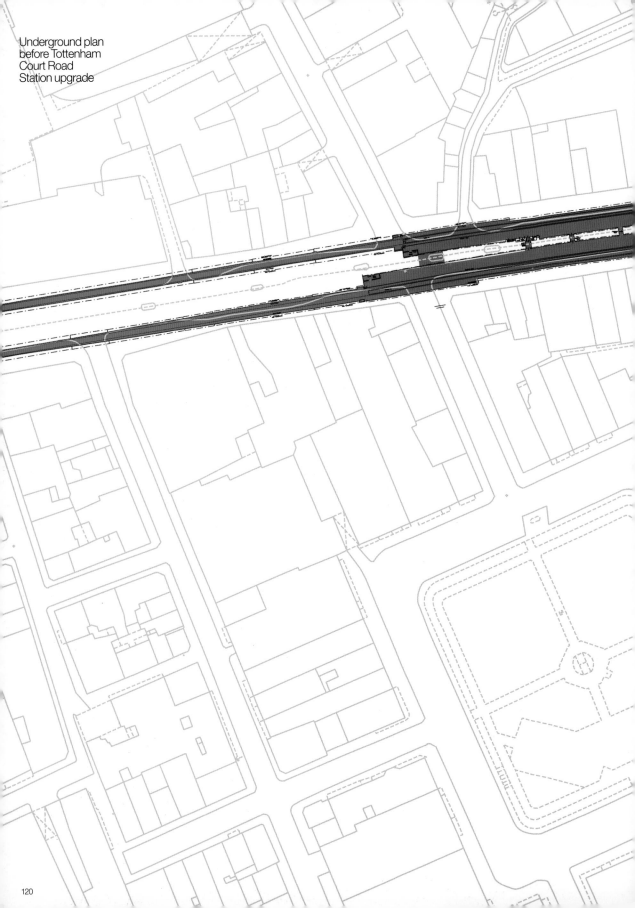

Underground plan
before Tottenham
Court Road
Station upgrade

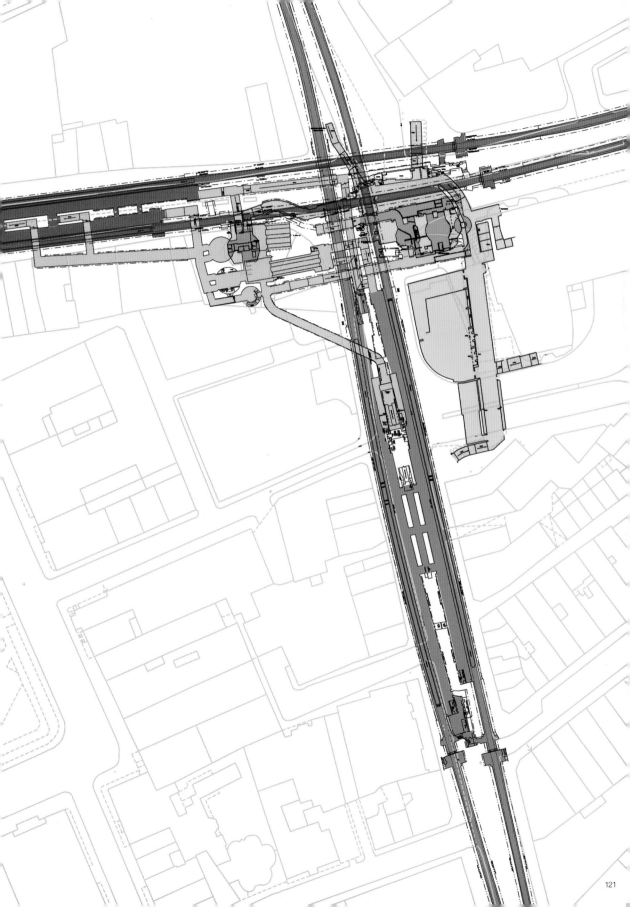

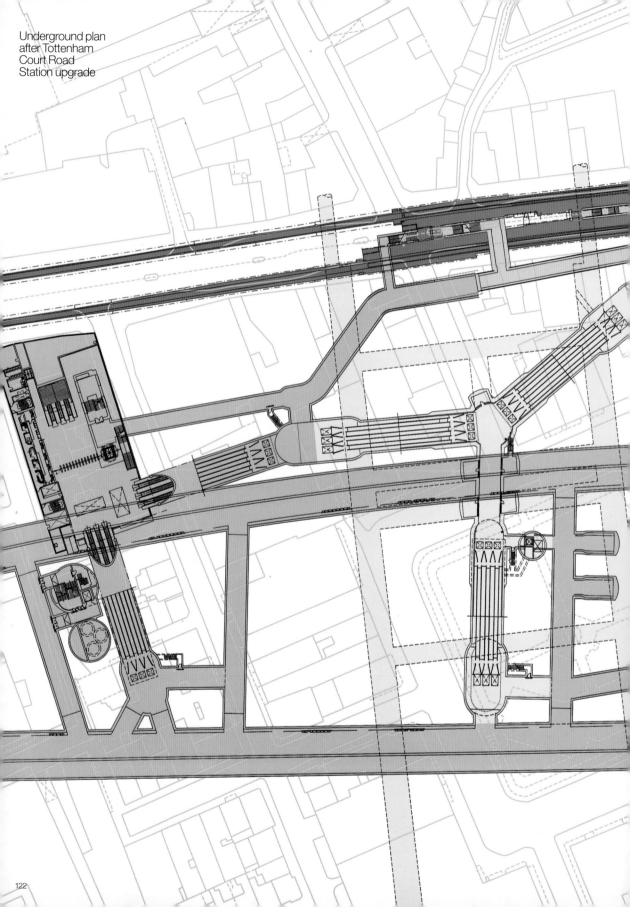

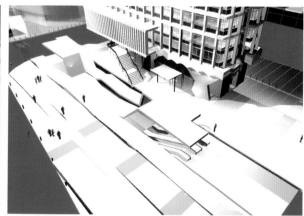

**Edwardian Buildings
Shoreditch Campus
Hackney Community
College, London**

Converted buildings retained as the
focus of the largest new further education
college in the UK.

community projects[1];
we do them;
we enjoy them;
they aren't easy;
we wave arms about in meetings;
wavy arms pay off;
in pockets of London;
where we've almost become;
4 projects later;
part of the community;

[1]Hackney Community College;
Trendy Hoxton was no-go-ville in 1996;

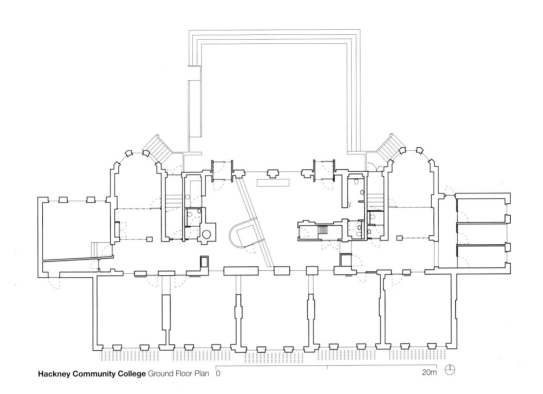

Hackney Community College Ground Floor Plan 0   20m

Section

Elevation

**Hackney Town Hall Square
Competition
London**

Response to a competition brief that
promoted publicity over architecture –
change of attitude without change to
the physical space.

invent something;
anything;
sew it into the project;
patent it;
and re-use it;
that word again;
be resourceful;
with words and ideas;
if you want a great idea, have lots of ideas;
as a pharmacist[1] once said;

[1]Linus Pauling, US Chemist, 1901–1994;

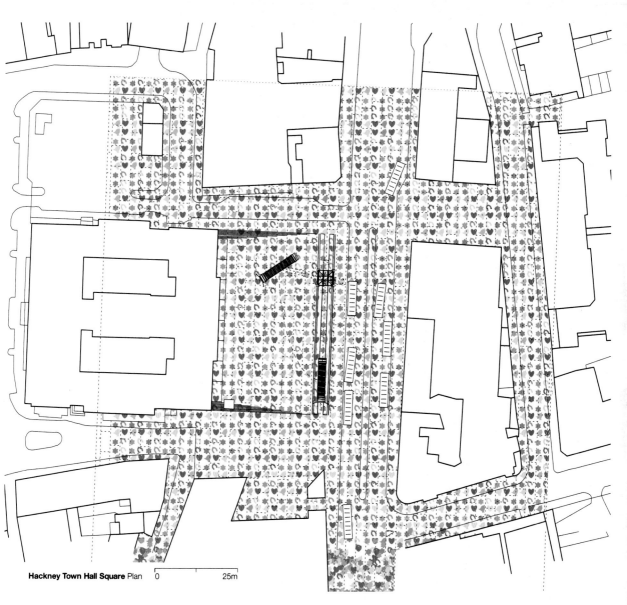

Hackney Town Hall Square Plan 0 _____ 25m

Confetti printed
flooring celebrating
weddings at the
Town Hall

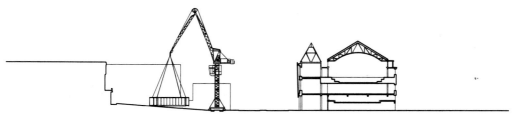

Section

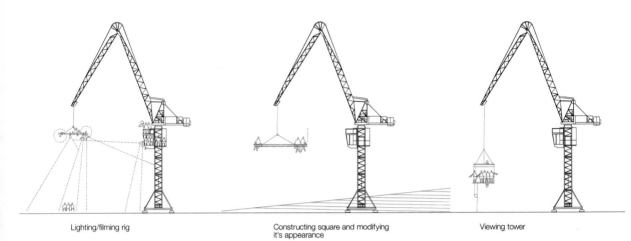

Lighting/filming rig

Constructing square and modifying
it's appearance

Viewing tower

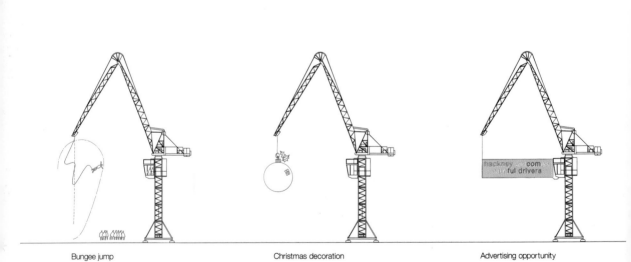

Bungee jump

Christmas decoration

Advertising opportunity

BELIEVE IN HACKNEY I
HACKNEY I BELIEVE IN
BELIEVE IN HACKNEY I
HACKNEY I BELIEVE IN
BELIEVE IN HACKNEY I
HACKNEY I BELIEVE IN
BELIEVE IN HACKNEY I
HACKNEY I BELIEVE IN
BELIEVE IN HACKNEY I
HACKNEY I BELIEVE IN
BELIEVE IN HACKNEY I
HACKNEY I BELIEVE IN
BELIEVE IN HACKNEY I
HACKNEY I BELIEVE IN

4
principles

Hawley Wharf
Camden

Regeneration of Camden Market as a
new retail destination mixed with studios,
workshops and flats around a public
performance space.

buildings must add value;
not in a monetary sense;
what it is worth is worthless;
nor worthy;
we cannot save the planet or the human race;
but worthwhile;
the importance of it to those who use it;
how they come to appreciate it;
inside and outside;
the difference it makes;
stop trying to be different;
just make a difference[1];

[1]Hawley Wharf;
Disused dregs of Camden Market;
Reborn as place to live, eat, drink, shop, sit and stare
at cascading canals;

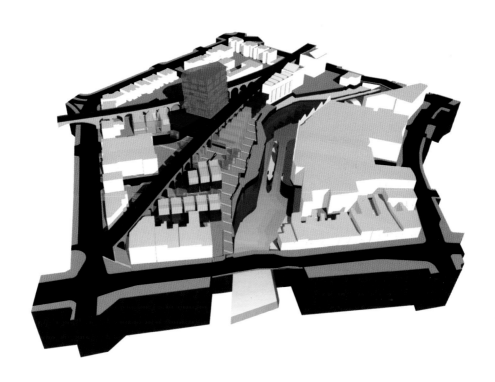

Making space for art
Julie Summers and Russell Brown

The concepts of art, the functions and aesthetics of art and the storage and presentation of art are all central to Hawkins\Brown's practice. But they are clear that art and architecture are two distinct disciplines with their own rules, restrictions and rewards. Art is generally free of practical and programmatic constraints, does not require that the artist engage with the capitalist system and can be entirely driven as a personal statement – offered to the world on a "take it or leave it" basis.

Architecture, by contrast is not an independent solitary process. Hawkins\Brown see it as critically linked, or more directly as, an expression of the influence of users, site, finance, timing and technical means. It is not independent of the means of self-expression, but then again it is not a truly 'social sculpture' or a form of public art. Any designer can imagine a 'virtual' space, draw it, model it, talk about it or write about it, but Hawkins\Brown strongly believe it does not become architecture until it enters the 'real' world, evidencing all the compromises and trials of realisation. Architecture is experienced by its users, by passers-by, or neighbours, and the building is changed and evolves through being inhabited.

That said, concepts and practices from art continually influence their practice. They describe the work of refurbishment in the same way that Miro asked people to come into his studio to mark a blank canvas so that he had something to react against in starting the creative process. Gigon Guyer describe the same process – "We function something like oysters that react to foreign bodies by producing pearls."

Hawkins\Brown describe the difficulty of finding a starting point for the design of the Student Centre at Portsmouth University, that is, until they accepted that the existing building on the site, Gun House, should stay and their new building could begin to shape itself against this fixed element, almost rub against its abrasiveness.

When designing an exhibition of architects paintings at the RIBA, Hawkins\Brown took Matisse's collage The Snail and organised the exhibition panels in the spiralling form of the artist's cut paper shapes – bringing two dimensional artwork into a three dimensional space.

In particular, Hawkins\Brown have been influenced by Joseph Beuys, Richard Long, Andrew Goldsworthy, Richard Wentworth and Rachel Whiteread, in whose work the materiality of the sculptural elements is highlighted. They provide research and attitudes that can be brought into the architectural process to refine and clarify a choice of materials, the manipulation of scale, or the foregrounding of specific elements.

Hawkins\Brown are continually feeding the exchange between artist and architect, always seeking to involve the artist(s) from the outset of a project. The basic concepts for a scheme are often checked through the eyes of the artist(s) – very different, purer and more radical, perhaps, than those of the architects. Themes addressed in a scheme can be expanded and clarified, with further possibilities being suggested.

Hawkins\Brown believe that artists are "further along" in perceiving the environment, more highly tuned to our cultural landscape, reacting more sensitively and swiftly to changes and shifts in the spirit of a place. Artists are able to call attention to different phenomena as sources of inspiration. It is interesting to note that over the past few decades art has developed more interesting strategies and has attracted more intellectual and creative people to it than the field of architecture. Artists are often more open to research, more interested in investigation than in defending their professional position. In this way their conceptual work is heightened, enriched, challenged and developed. The artist is interested in working with big, popular ideas and large dimensions – really changing the way people perceive a place – taking risks. Process is as important to the artist as the final result.

At the Henry Moore Foundation Hawkins\Brown have focussed their attention for the past ten years on the complex series of buildings that form the sculptor's estate in Perry Green, Hertfordshire. All of the buildings on the site were either placed or procured by Moore and his personality and compositional eye is tangible throughout the grouping of studios, workshops, storage buildings external spaces and offices for the Foundation's curators and staff. The challenge here was to take a series of disparate and self contained elements and unite them into a whole that not only reflects Moore's sensibility of what was appropriate in the countryside but managed the legacy, the personalities and the expectations of those who worked with Moore when he was alive. By using a limited palette of refined materials and making simple recognisable forms to contain, at times, quite complicated programmatic requirements, the thorny issues of image and longevity were bypassed. What resulted was a timeless architecture that is both adaptable and pleasurable.

A more radical example of the dialogue between artist and architect was the "I beLIeVE IN HACKNEY" project. The Council in Hackney needed to find a way to develop Hackney Town Hall Square as the centre of a new cultural quarter. Hawkins\Brown chose to work with Andrew Cross and the artist Bob and Roberta Smith. In the proposal submitted to Hackney Council, Hawkins\Brown wrote "I BELIEVE IN HACKNEY is a statement of belief in the regeneration of Hackney. Although simple as a phrase, it expresses the key to a cultural regeneration that architecture cannot provide alone." The project was approached with wit and humour but the message was serious: Hackney required a wider cultural identity in order to attract investment and to encourage public participation in its regeneration.

A painting brandishing the slogan "I BELIEVE IN HACKNEY", by Bob and Roberta Smith, was the starting point for this rebranding. The team recognised that the square was a vital axis through which bus routes linked Hackney with every part of London. This suggested that buses could carry posters of "I BELIEVE IN HACKNEY" to a much wider audience. An I BELIEVE IN HACKNEY store selling I BELIEVE IN HACKNEY products was conceived, as a 'pavement of business' – encouraging the involvement of small local businesses in the scheme.

The reorientation of the square and the construction of a gently sloping surface to transform it into a stage was intended to "suggest a more democratic approach for the local authority". The Council was split in its reaction to the scheme but some councillors felt that Hawkins\Brown had got to the heart of Hackney and that the solution was innovative and exciting. The more conservative councillors, however, won the day with their preference for a more "civic" scheme, with sculpture and fountains. Nothing has happened.

The I BELIEVE IN HACKNEY project was critical in the practice's understanding of the potential for collaboration between artist and architect. Hawkins\Brown realised that these dialogues are fundamental to a creative design process. What had begun at the Henry Moore Foundation and UCE became radicalised in the Hackney project and is now a central theme of Hawkins\Brown's approach to any project.

At the University of Portsmouth Hawkins\Brown asked Martin Richman to collaborate in making an artwork that was integral to the architecture of the new Student Centre. Richman was born in Southsea and had vivid childhood memories of the lights on the pier and the boats in its harbour. As a student he studied at Portsmouth College of Art and after a career working in lighting design for the music and theatre industries he has become a well-known 'light artist'. Although he lives and works in London his childhood images of lights were a starting point for the scheme at the Student Centre where he created a huge light box, which sits on top of the new building, sending out pulsing light into the surrounding streets. The play of light is an important feature of the building, both in terms of the legibility of the interior spaces – marking the entrance, for example – and representing the uses of the building as a nightclub. However, Richman's sculptural light box goes further than merely providing a new beacon of light on the Portsmouth skyline, it houses the extensive plant for the major venue that is the centre space of the scheme, it sends out a message of vibrant life within – as much an advertisement as a symbol. The success of this collaboration is that it works on all levels, with the building being enriched by the link between the client, artist, architect and city. Such a link could not have been forged without the artist's conceptual input and the sensitive handling of his ideas in the architecture.

As part of a larger regeneration scheme, Hawkins\Brown are designing a new public space in Dalston, East London – Gillett Square. Andrew Cross and Hawkins\Brown have continued their dialogue, initiated with the I BELIEVE IN HACKNEY campaign. Their conversations have taken place whilst walking the streets of Hackney, away from the architect's offices or artist's studio. Cross was attracted to the project for several reasons. "On the one hand", he wrote in the proposal, "collaborative teamwork… provides an interesting contrast to the relatively solitary practice of the artist. Working on a project with Hawkins\Brown which does not bear the stamp of an individual identity…" Another aspect he looked forward to is: "Hawkins\Brown create new architectural forms but they are not concerned solely within the legacy of signature statements." This collaboration is being assisted by the Royal Society of Arts with an Art for Architecture grant.

The commercial scheme to the north of the square has involved a whole group of artists through Hales Gallery and their curator/entrepreneur Paul Hedge. He has been involved from the outset of the design process suggesting venues, forms, materials or conceptual approaches for the emerging elements of the building. The end result is still unpredictable but is likely to include a three storey 60m long painting on acrylic by Danny Rolph, installations by Hans Op de Beeck and Andrew Bick. Each flat within the scheme will have original stencils printed on the walls by a group of artists, sold as a work of art along with the lease of the flats.

Paul Hedge has described the process as "curating the whole building" or designing an art museum rather than a housing scheme.

One of the clearest points emerging from any examination of Hawkins\Brown's processes is the positive approach they take towards collaboration. Engaging others, including artists, helps define a special quality in their work. In foregoing, to some extent, the long tradition of the importance placed on the individual power of the architect they are subsuming it for the sake of a broader collective approach.

As with all the projects in the office, Hawkins\Brown are often seeking allusive, poetic or non-abstract responses to very practical problems. They believe that artistic ideas can often communicate in a more viable language than the restricted/heuristic readings of modern architecture.

Hawkins\Brown actively seek inspiration and parallels in art because it offers an alternative route out of and transcends the narrow architectural preoccupations of form making, style, technical virtuosity and offers liberating contact with the big, populist questions of "Who are we?", "Why we are here?" and "What defines us?"

TAKE IT ON THE BEACH AND LET SAND GATHER IN THE SPINE.

The Henry Moore
Foundation
Much Hadham
Hertfordshire

Sensitive completion and adaptation
to a series of buildings that house the
Foundation – metamorphosis from
old to new.

buildings respond;
they're a reflex action;
to a social context;
triggered;
by a need, a want, a wish;
once built;
we respond to them;
man to wall to man;
a game of wallie;
only slower[1];

[1] The sheep grazing around and muttering to the Sheep Field Barn Gallery;
The Henry Moore Foundation;
Much Hadham, England;

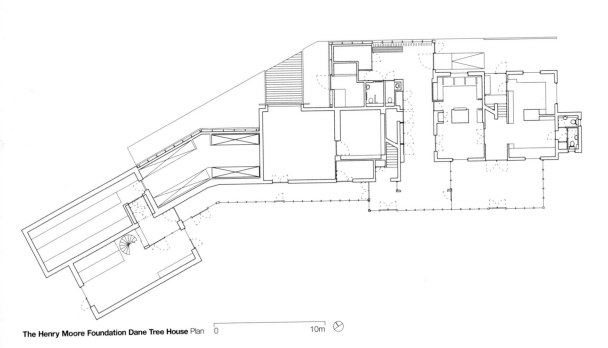

The Henry Moore Foundation Dane Tree House Plan   0   10m

figures;
easy to impress;
square tonnage;
millions of poundage;
how many awardsage;
figures are stats;
stats are rational;
the language of mathematicians;
the most vital measure;
is people¹;

To date, 12,000,000+ people have passed
through Hawkins\Brown buildings;
At least 33 animals too;

BUILDINGS HELP PEOPLE. WHEN DID YOU LAST HELP A BUILDING?

First

Ground

Open exhibition space

Closed exhibition space

The Henry Moore
Foundation Alternative
layout options
Not to scale

Northeast Elevation

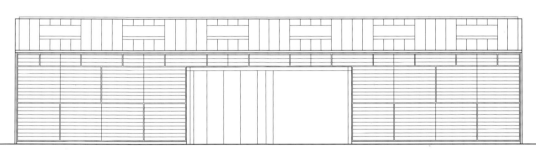

The Henry Moore Foundation Northwest Elevation

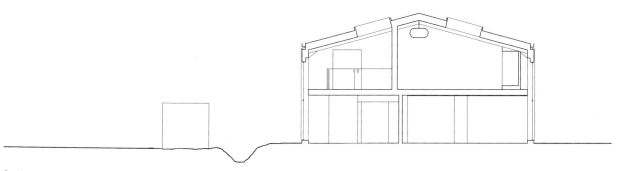

Section

Avenue Campus
Faculty of Arts
University of Southampton

Redevelopment of Edwardian school and
playing fields to create a new Arts Faculty.

context vs use;
they needn't fight;
take turns to lead;
what a building might be;
can change;
and adapt;
and/or multiply;
but where it is is where it is;
what's around it is what's around it;
and even they can change too;
nothing's permanent;
all is flux;

Avenue Campus, Faculty of Arts, University of Southampton;
Studied which people worked where;
Took a loose-fit, long-life approach;

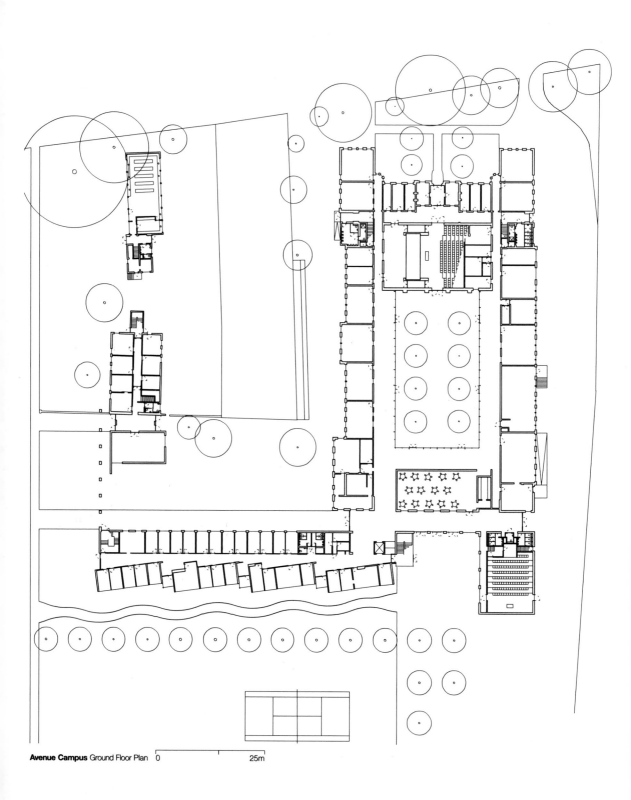

Avenue Campus Ground Floor Plan   0   25m

West Elevation

East Elevation

5
economy

New School of Healthcare
Oxford Brookes University

Bringing the three departments of nursing,
physiotherapy and occupational health
from nine sites together for the first time
in a totally flexible new building.

don't make buildings big;
make them useful;
so people use them;
some call it sustainability;
we call it logic;
more space gets used;
more of the time';
and the building ends up littler;
or the room you're in;
feels 3 times the size;

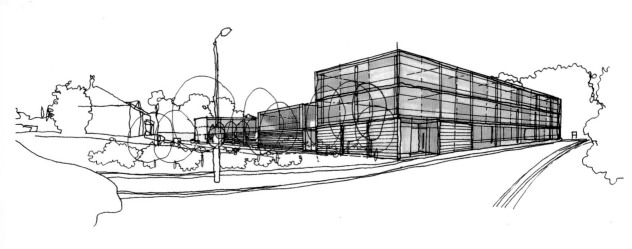

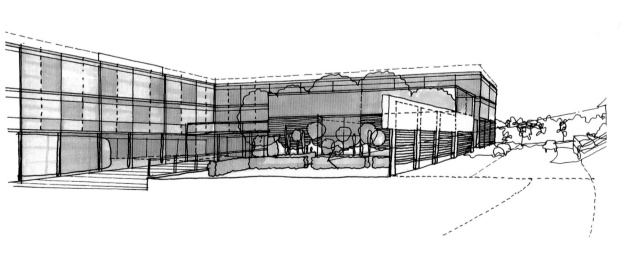

Student Union Association Building Queen Mary University of London

Complicated building process –
reconfiguring the Union, bar, venue and
shops. Simplifying the whole building
to create a new public image.

wastefulness pollutes the industry;
so much single use;
sole selfish owners;
space is democratic;
why not share;
embrace duality;
climb into bed with triality;
play twister with quadality;
one day maybe mass centality;
a hundred uses;
never a bored day for a building[1];

[1]Student Union Association Building,
Queen Mary, University of London;
£1.3 million project done in 10 week Summer Break;
Students return in disbelief;

174

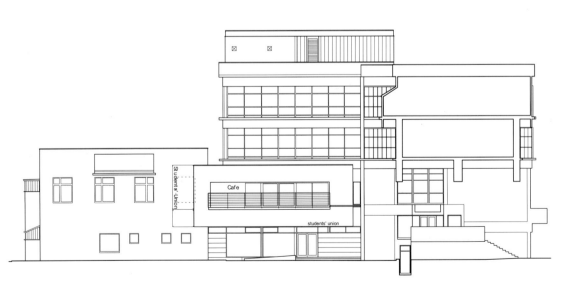

Queen Mary, University of London Elevation

IS A LANDMARK SOMEWHERE WHERE PEOPLE WANT TO BE PHOTOGRAPHED?

New Business School
University of Portsmouth

A new business school and a school
for new business.

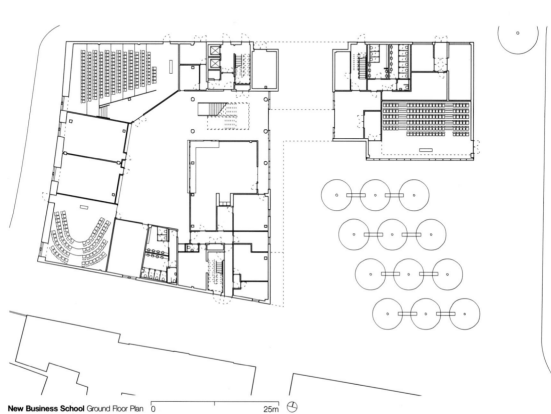

New Business School Ground Floor Plan 0   25m

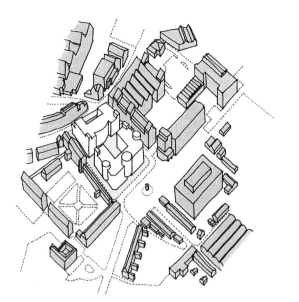

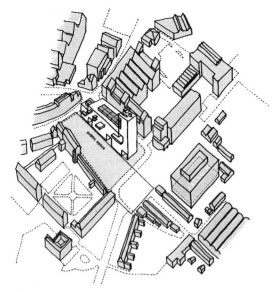

1 Planning Scheme: The Sandcastle
 (+ve)
– Maximises available area

 (-ve)
– Little contextual response
– No room for expansion
– Feels like two separate buildings
– No gesture/generosity towards public space
– No character
– Access to rear building via first floor bridge

2 Wall building
 (+ve)
– Lots of sunny public space
– Tower creates focus at point of access
– Very responsive to context

 (-ve)
– Building fails to engage existing public space at Lion Terrace
– New public space has wrong focus

Competition stage
development
analysis for
Portsmouth
Business School

frugality;
is sensibility;
from little money grows ingenuity;
more fun on a budget;
think of it as our money[1];
suddenly;
it's all so easy;
not to squander;
not to patronise;
not to be kitsch;

[1]New Business School, Portsmouth;
300 seat lecture theatre and seminar zones wrapped
around central light well;
Radically low energy use;

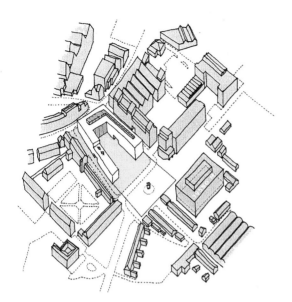

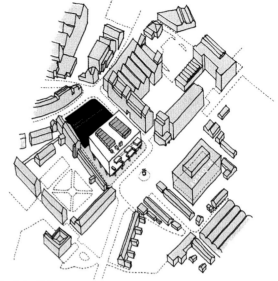

3 Horseshoe building

(+ve)
– Creates a shared, sheltered public space

(-ve)
– No real frontage
– Single point of entry makes for excessive circulation space
– Confused identity
– Does not respond to scale of existing buildings at rear

4 Block building

(+ve)
– Frees up half of the site for future development
– Plus away from low-rise Georgian houses at rear
– Prominent frontage at point of arrival
– Resolves the problem of Purbeck St

(-ve)
– Block form too high against milldam building
– Rik of over-development when site at rear is used
– Hides school of architecture from public space

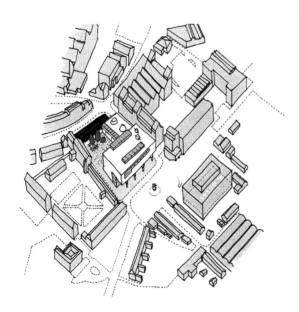

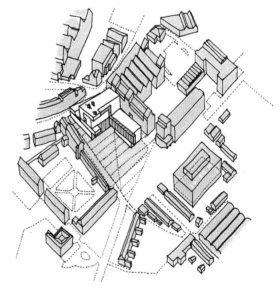

5 Bridge building

(+ve)
– Allows for 'garden'
– Scale responds to surrounding fabric at rear
– Allows reduced space for future development
– Potential to reinforce historic route in courtyards

(-ve)
– Access to rear wing at first floor only via bridge link

6 Corner building

(+ve)
– Engages exiting public space at lion terrace
– Responds contextually to the surrounding buildings
– Form of building signifies the entrance
– Building provides an iconic identity for the school
– Courtyards at front and rear capture the sun
– Predominant north-south orientation minimises energy use

(-ve)
– Limited potential for future developments

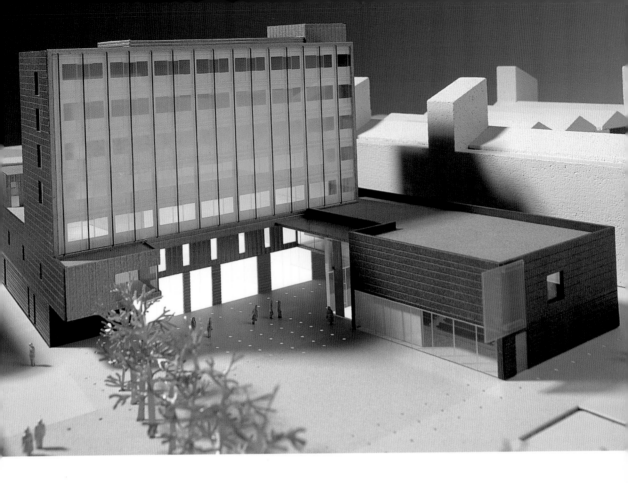

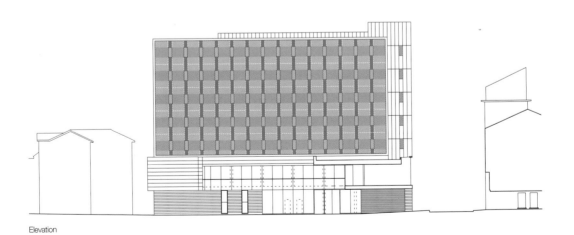

Elevation

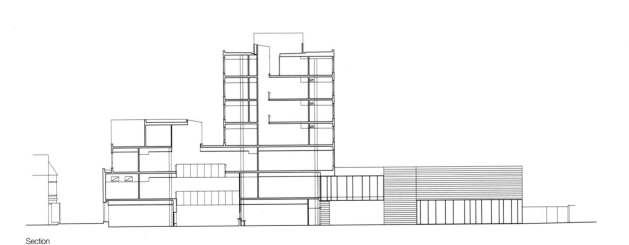

Section

Opus One
Anglia Polytechnic University
Cambridge

Redevelopment of outdated Sixties campus
fitting a new music school, arts centre and
teaching spaces to create
a new court.

Sifting';
now there's a good verb;
so sift we do;
for what's good;
and what's bad;
what to throw away;
and how to dispose of it;
or should we recycle;
it's 'also' again;
back to front and;
upside down and;
inside out;

Anglia Polytechnic University's green travel policy;
Downsize car park;
Upsize education;
Pedestrianised courtyards linked by 'streets';
New homes for music therapy, pharmacy, IT and the Arts;

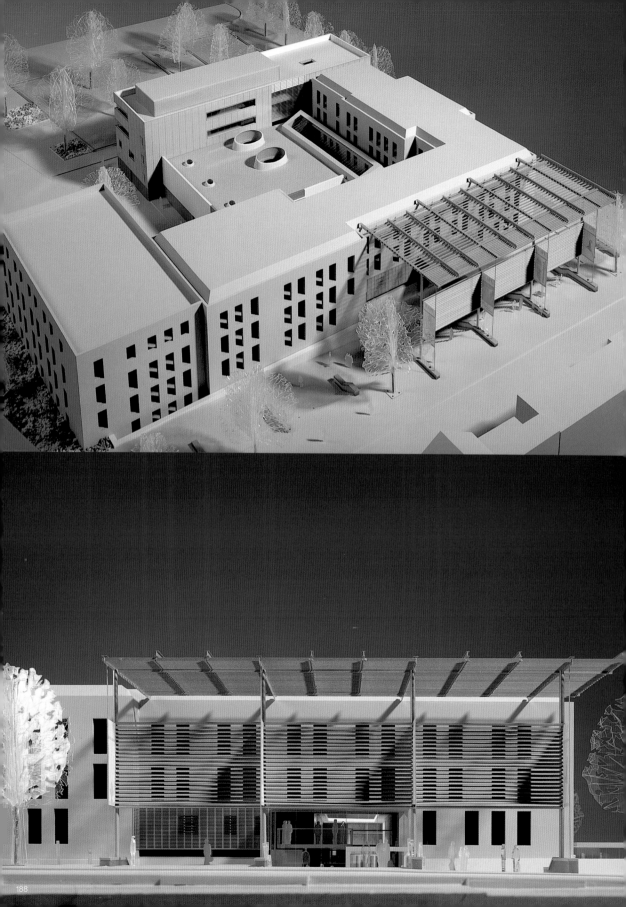

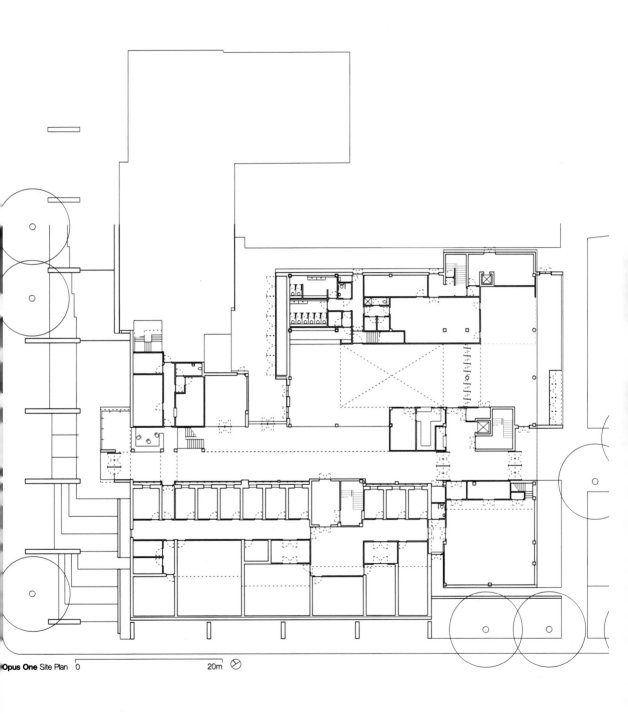

Opus One Site Plan

0   20m

6
industry

Hope (Sufferance) Wharf
Rotherhithe

Groundbreaking residential development
of a series of listed buildings.

ROTHERHITHE WORKSHOPS

HOPE (SUFFERANCE) WHARF

HOPE (

arrogance annoys us;
architects ooze arrogance;
tearing down good buildings;
because it's easier to design from new;
zero sensitivity;
be the building;
understand why it's there;
it's older than us[1];
it's wiser than us;
it's lived more life;
respect the permanence;

[1]Hope (Sufferance) Wharf;
Listed building;
Helped by Planning Authority and English Heritage;
Thames-side housing that reveres its landlord;

Hope (Sufferance) Wharf Site Plan 0 ⊢————————————⊣ 10m ⊕

Section

Elevation

2–10 Hertford Road
London

A megastructure that develops the debate as to how we mix new models of living and working.

architects are not brands;
brands are merely image;
brands don't exist;
they're invisible;
they're invented[1];
buildings created architects;
not the other way round;
thank god we need shelter;
shelter gives us jobs;
ta god;

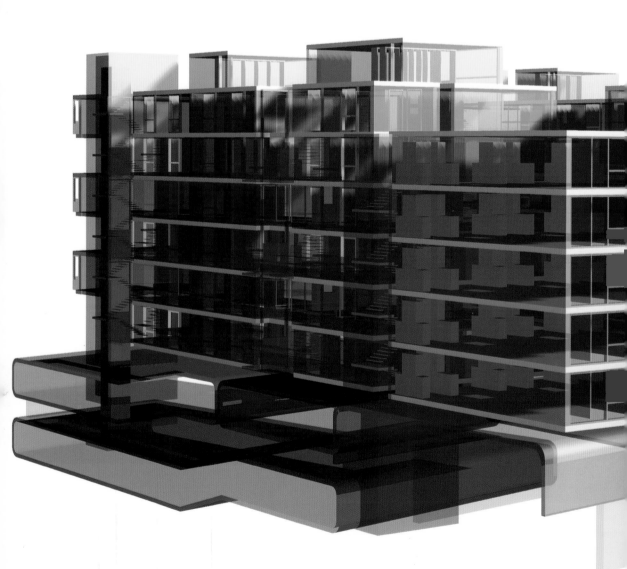

[1]Created SODA (South of Dalston);
New community beside the canal;
Lifted mood of whole area;
Hertford Road, Hackney;

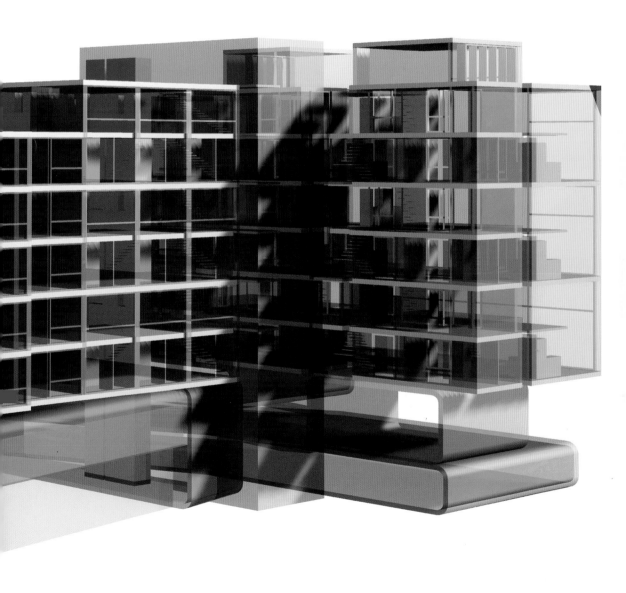

is excitable water
² hawkins\brown

Hawkins\Brown
branding concepts
for new district –
SODA

sohonotoriousboutiquehotelillicitsexdrugsrockandrollsubvoyeurcashfromchaoscafefilmpinkpoundinglibertycommunityredlightglitterballtheatrecruisemediasquarelost?yuareherestreetbritartindustryoilfilmcanalloftkylieraunchgrittyillicitcashfromcacheurbanchickeyfloatstarsecretcommunitylegendarysoda

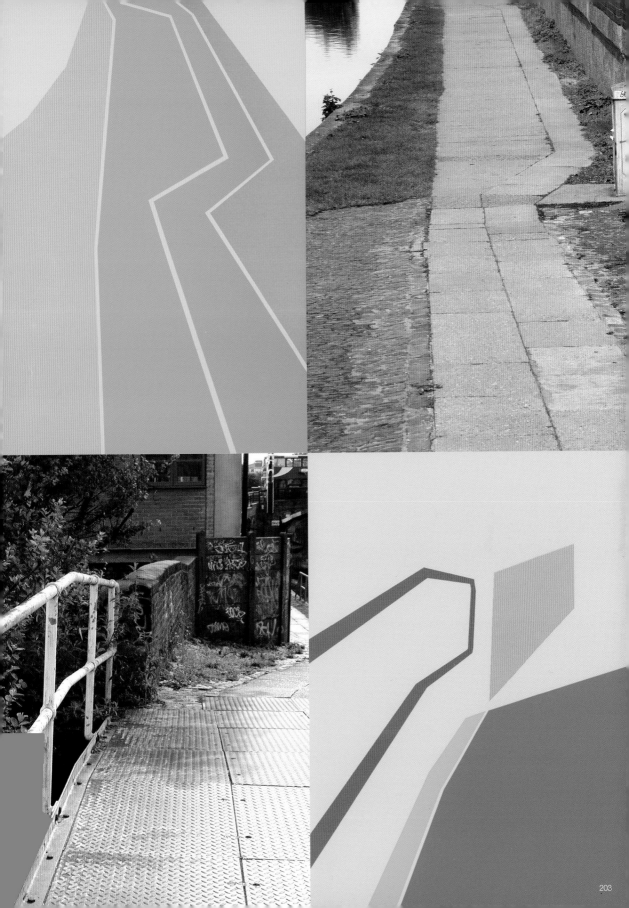

STOP READING AFTER 32 MINUTES WHETHER YOU ARE BORED OR INTERESTED.

VISIT THIS BUILDING BY TUBE AND RETURN BY BUS, WHISTLING.

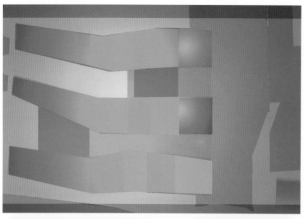
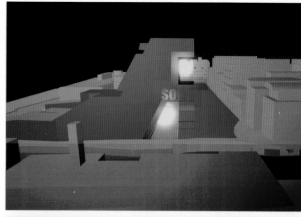
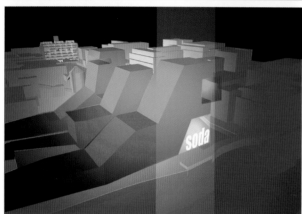
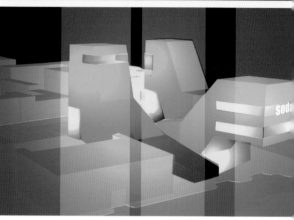
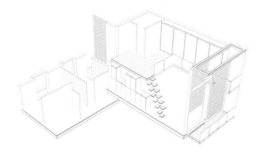
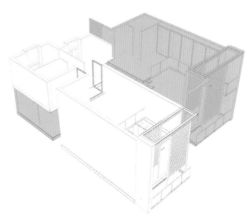
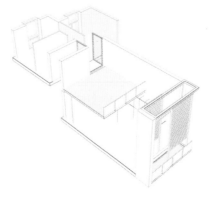

we are not architects;
a job title is a red herring;
something to hide behind;
like a grey suit;
better be who we really are;
people who design buildings;
letting style follow purpose;
bin the ego;
and the letters after the name;
and the business card that says architect;

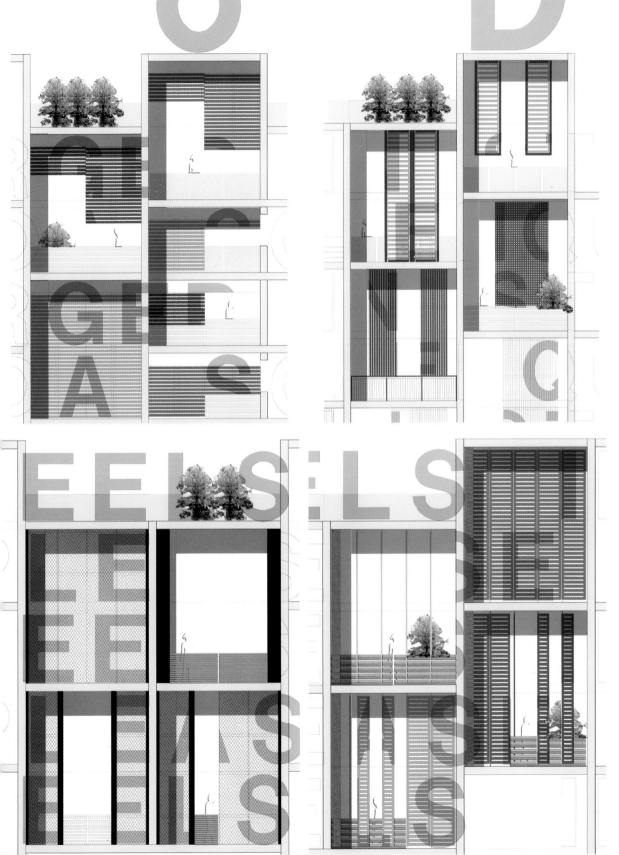

11–23 Downham Road
London

Labyrinth like structure collecting studios, workspace, flats, live/ workspaces in response to a complex urban environment.

we're misfits;
in an anal world;
of this is this and can't be that;
well, we are that;
the other;
rather than just another;
we mix our work;
who wouldn't want to work with diverse groups[1];
harder to pigeonhole;
when you're free-range;

[1]Mixed use dense terrace;
Community initiated workspace, café and education centre;
Scissor section flats link front to back;
Downham Road, Hackney;

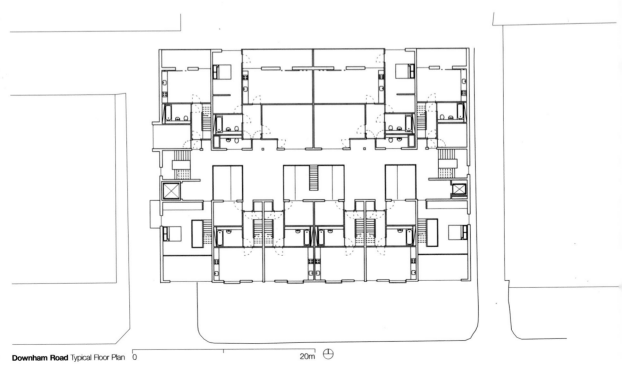

Downham Road Typical Floor Plan 0   20m

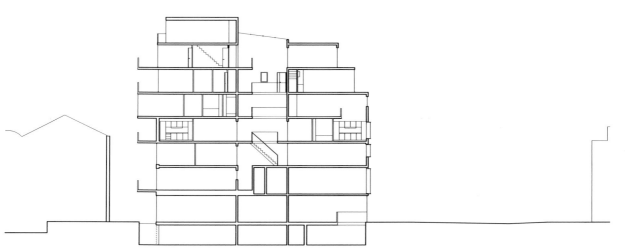

Section

The Billiard Hall
West Bromwich

Applying a unique attitude to colour to
a standard commercial model – clever
and populist at the same time.

beware the men in black;
graphite cloaked coolies;
masking a fear;
of colour;
undertakers outdress architects;
colours change moods[1];
that's what we build;
moods;
give a place a vibe;
agitate the endorphins;
let colour boogie;
space is just a dancefloor;
waiting to be filled;

[1]The Billiard Hall, West Bromwich;
Multi-coloured design in a multi-cultural district;
Wins CAMRA pub conversion of the year award;

7
optimism

Trowbridge Centre
for Adults with
Learning Difficulties

A long-term relationship with a building
with an unhappy history that has slowly
turned itself into a place for all the
community to meet.

back of beyond;
places no-one wants to see;
these are the gems;
that motivate;
bleak beginnings;
where we plant catalysts;
the first flag[1];
then ripples of opportunity;
radiate out;
bringing people in[2];
this is how religion works;

[1]Day-glo pink roof sculpture;
Trowbridge estate;
Hackney back alleys;

[2]3 metre high Makaton sculpture;
Makaton is sign language used by those with learning difficulties;
Trowbridge Centre for Adults with Learning Difficulties, Hackney;

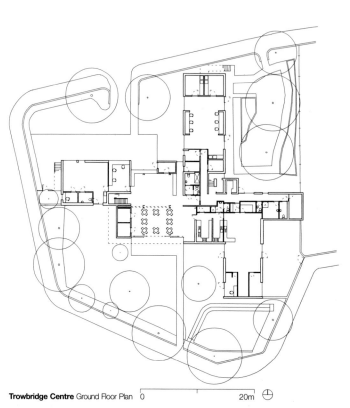

Trowbridge Centre Ground Floor Plan 0 20m

love the underdog;
if there's not a true problem;
a moral spark-plug;
it's hard to do it just for the money;
or prestige;
there's enough people in that bunfight;
unequal opportunities;
are where the real deal is;
that's not to say;
we wouldn't build an airport;
if asked;

WHEN NECK ACHES AND EYES REDDEN, STOP READING IMMEDIATELY, ESPECIALLY IF YOU ARE DRIVING.

Maggie's Cancer Care Centre Sheffield

Innovative national facility that deals holistically with cancer.

hope[1];
turns up when you give up;
build a place of hope;
that's not a church;
or a synagogue;
but a mild upper;
little stabs of optimism;
for disenchanted youth;
the unemployed;
are the future employers;
given the right oomph;

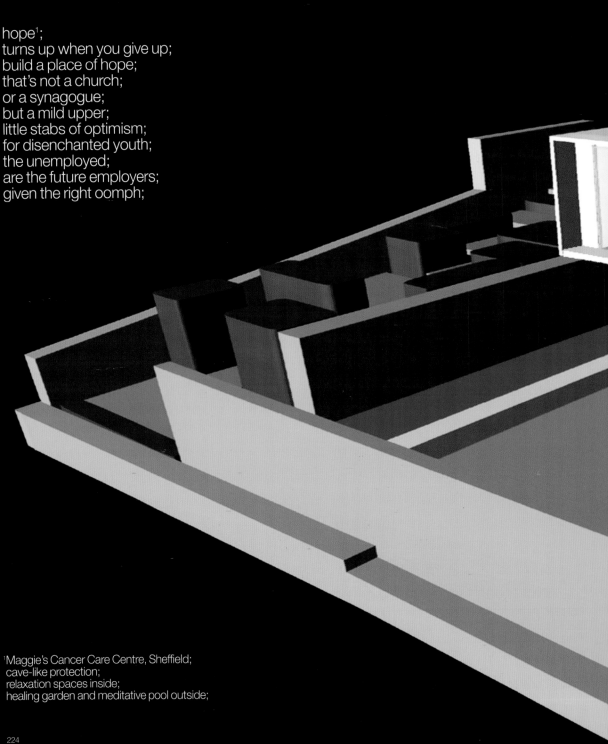

[1]Maggie's Cancer Care Centre, Sheffield;
cave-like protection;
relaxation spaces inside;
healing garden and meditative pool outside;

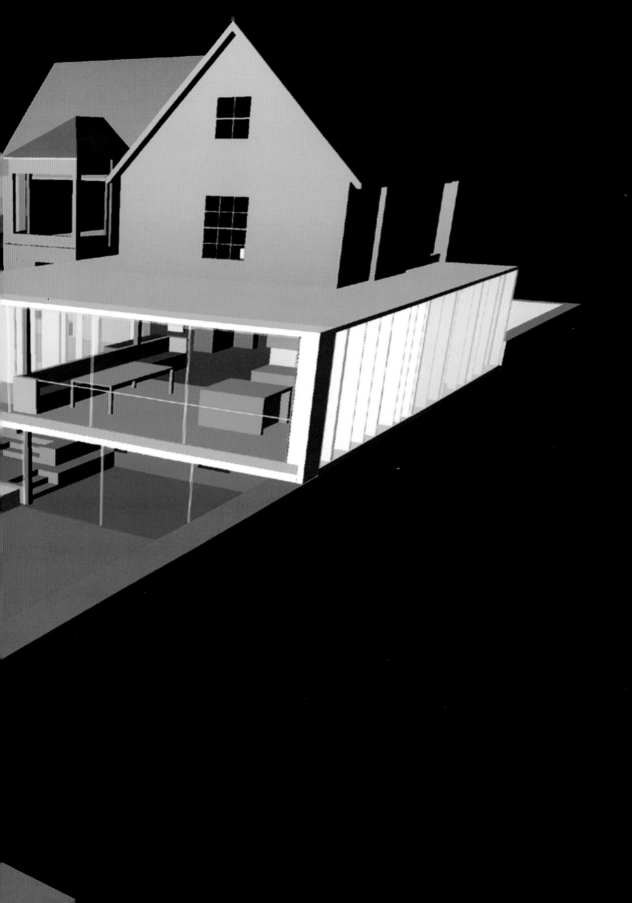

Long Library at
Sissinghurst used
as a reference for
initial competition
presented to
Charles Jencks

embrace failure[1];
it's no monster;
just the chance to learn;
what's scary about that;
failure out-teaches success;
all the accolades in the world;
make for a cautious practice;
afraid to fail;
and lose their mantel;
failing's fantastic;

[1]Ever tried. Ever failed. No matter. Try again. Fail again. Fail better;
Samuel Beckett;
Westward Ho;
A closed space novel;

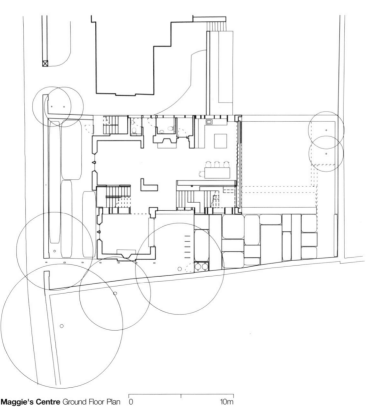

Maggie's Centre Ground Floor Plan   0   10m

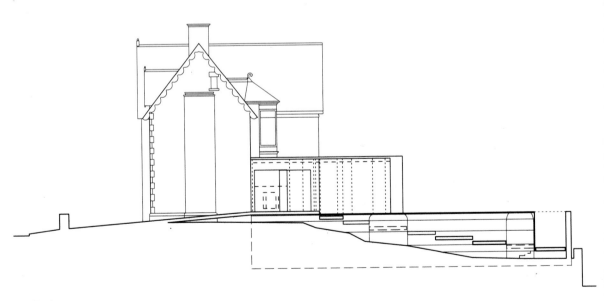

West Elevation

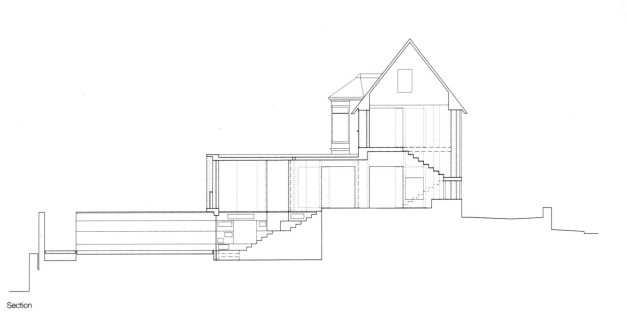

Section

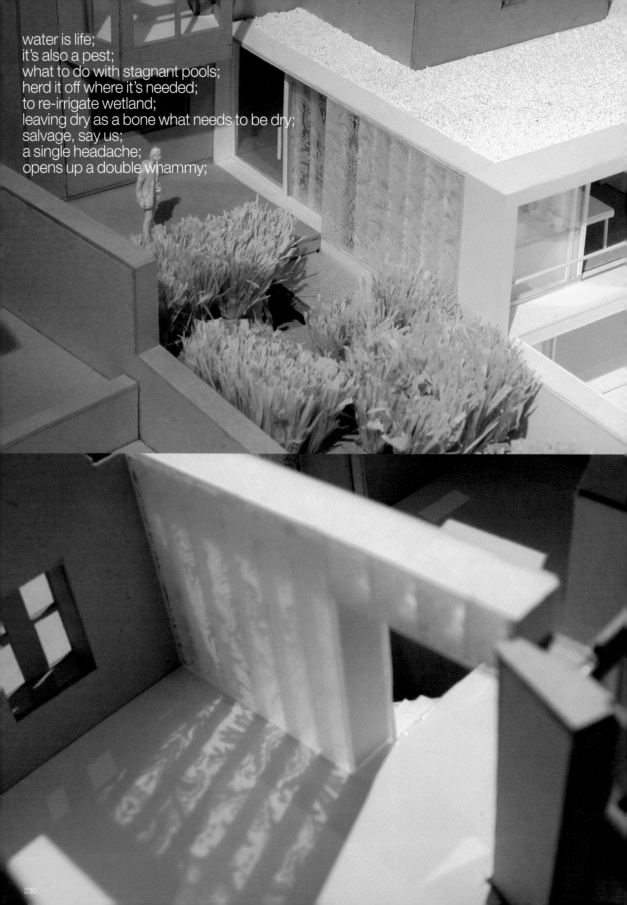

water is life;
it's also a pest;
what to do with stagnant pools;
herd it off where it's needed;
to re-irrigate wetland;
leaving dry as a bone what needs to be dry;
salvage, say us;
a single headache;
opens up a double whammy;

EARLY IN THE MORNING, GO TO THE BUILDING OF YOUR CHOICE AND GRAFFITI A SMALL ELEPHANT.

8
periphery

St Mary's Square
Bury St Edmunds

Reinterpreting a classic modernist house type against the backdrop of a medieval walled garden.

do planners plan[1];
or protract;
sometimes stalling helps;
sometimes it stumbles;
suppressing spontaneity;
tap-tackling momentum;
but recall;
how long it takes to train;
seven years;
we're a patient bunch;

[1] St Marys Square, Bury St Edmunds;
Planners OK'd extra storey on mews houses in conservation area;
Tardis-like homes radiate light and space;
Hailed modern classics;
At Housing Design Awards, "it does not qualify, but I want one";

WE'RE ALL DECIDUOUS. TREES, BUILDINGS, PEOPLE.

"does not qualify (but I want one)";
awards assessor;
The Housing Design Awards;
1998;

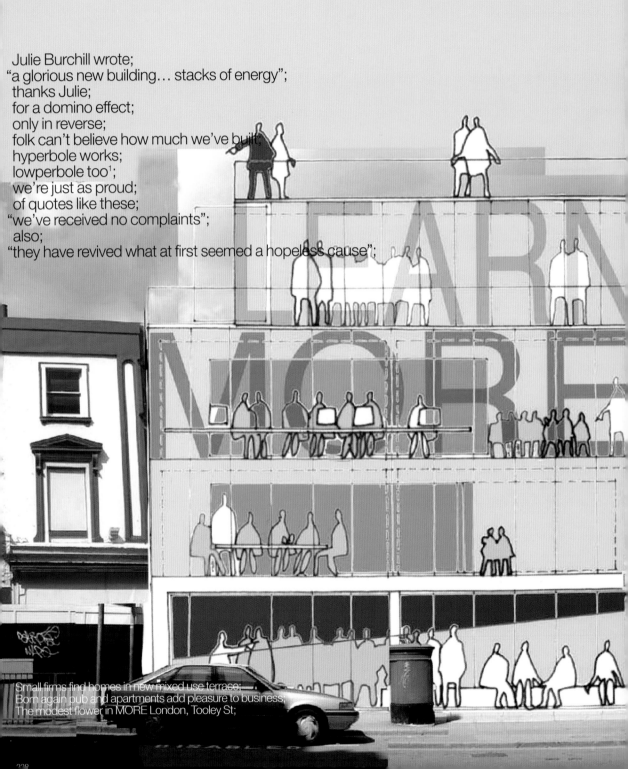

3–17 Tooley St

Mediating between the scale and
activities of the busy new office
site and the surrounding residential
neighbourhood with a new form
of library.

Julie Burchill wrote;
"a glorious new building… stacks of energy";
thanks Julie;
for a domino effect;
only in reverse;
folk can't believe how much we've built;
hyperbole works;
lowperbole too[1];
we're just as proud;
of quotes like these;
"we've received no complaints";
 also;
"they have revived what at first seemed a hopeless cause";

Small firms find homes in new mixed use terrace;
Born again pub and apartments add pleasure to business;
The modest flower in MORE London, Tooley St;

skateboarding;
what's our view;
if they skate fine;
if they don't skate fine;
our view on skateboarding;

Right: Townscape
analysis for Tooley
St Terrace

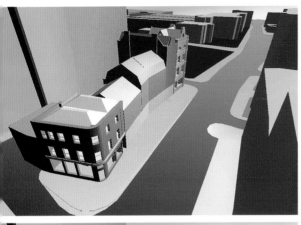
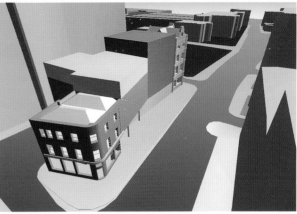

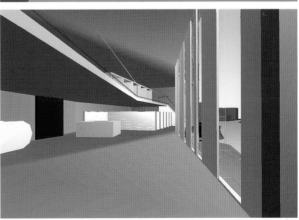

The Roald Dahl Centre

A museum for the writer and a literacy centre for children.

compliments;
hard to give, harder to take;
without the feet leaving the ground;
but exquisitely lovely;
when they hail from the hearts of innocents[1];
or the aesthetic shyness;
of councillors[2], dear of 'em;
and the unconscious compliment;
not even knowing it's happening[3];
praise;
always adored;
forever underrated;

[1]Roald Dahl Centre, Great Missenden, Bucks;
Place to simulate chaotic creativity in children;
And a museum to stabilise culture;

[2]Hackney Town Hall Square;
Pop in and make your own mind up;

[3]42–44 Beak Street;
Bought by Ridley Scott;
Became a media building;
Ended up on Film 92 with Barry Norman;

CHOOSE ONE WINDOW IN THIS BOOK THAT YOU WOULD WANT YOUR ASHES THROWN FROM.

Drawing out
the language of
the existing site
at Great Missenden

urban souk[1];
inner city renaissance brotherhood[2];
the Frank Zappa of architecture[3];
eclectic engineers[4];
many a label;
slapped upon us;
beware;
the media ain't mightier than word-of-mouth;

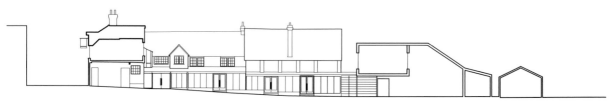

Elevation

Section

[1]Critic unknown;

[2]Is this you Brian Sewell?;

[3]We made this one up and just want to be associated with a genius;

[4]The clients who said we were confused when all we are is curious;

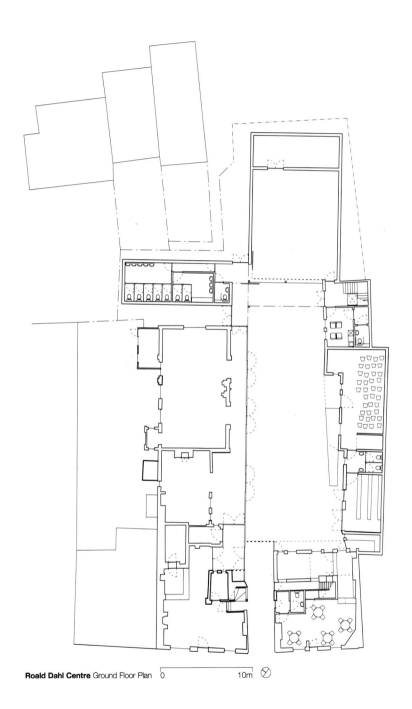

Roald Dahl Centre Ground Floor Plan 0   10m ⊗

Context and proposition:
two approaches to the siting
of the work of Hawkins\Brown
Kevin Rhowbotham

Part One
A proposed architectural context
to the work of Hawkins\Brown

Aspects of a contemporary programmatic

Not for some considerable time have architects turned their attentions towards the thorny issues raised by conditions of use. Indeed it must be more than fair to say that, certainly, since the late 1960s, architects have been driven by issues concerned primarily with conditions of form and of form making. I mean by this that they have concerned themselves with those aspects of architectural production which fall beyond the realm of use, beyond what was referred to by the modernist faction as function and which in more contemporary circles has now been termed programme.

Since the 60s form and use have been divided. This dividing is not however, a condition of exclusion, such that form has excluded use, but rather a condition of authority, such that form and form making have dominated the intellectual researches of the architectural fringe, retaining issues of use as merely a foil to the primary work.

This shift in the intellectual affections of architects reflected a general intellectual shift in the West, away from materialist instrumentalism towards a new idealism and to an affection for form, pattern and structure. It also brought with it a keen interest in diversity and complexity which from the outset had intrigued post war architects and encouraged the best of them to seek wider anthropologically diverse approaches to conditions of inhabitation and use. The Smithsons, Aldo Van Eyck, and Herman Herzberger established a social dimension and a new programmatic in which relevant social patterns could be examined as the basis of a programmatically driven architecture. This nascent social formalism was relatively short lived however, countered at the end of the 60s by the radical materialism of the Situations International and its popular representation by Archigram. The mature and patient research of the Dutch Structuralist school, as it has since been erroneously named, derived in large part from the CIAM tradition, could not be sustained in the face of a single issue architecture. Concerns for complex problems of inhabitation, mass housing and social provision across the social spectrum proved less enticing than concerns for the temporary or moving architectures which had an immediate popular appeal fed by a spectacular graphic style.

It would not have proved so inimical to the state of architectural programmatics had a single issue formalism retained any political dimension. One harbours a distinct suspicion, however, that most of its appeal derived precisely from this fact. What followed is well documented, and usually in glowing terms, but a comprehensive · understanding of precisely how the contemporary city is used, fell short of the postmodern project in all its guises; neo-classical, neo-rationalist and neo-suprematist. From Ungers to Rossi, from Hadid to Eisenman issues of space were constructed from formal paradigms often collated from separate compositional traditions. Aspects of a socio-political analysis were understood to be of no particular relevance and part of the concerns of a previous generation of architects. The articulation and research of programmatic use found no champions during this period.

Commercial development, on the other hand, was quick to claim new programmatic territories and to see the importance and relevance of new data collection techniques in order to improve and expand its business concerns. The hyper-mall and the theme park, a kind of pragmatic topographical demography of retail and leisure consumerism, were established, as the primary shibboleths of late twentieth century development culture, without a hint of prissiness. As workload shifted from commercial office to commercial retail, no corresponding intellectual shift followed. This shift, either misread or dismissed by the discipline in general was considered irrelevant to its predominantly formal concerns. It remained unexamined by the leading thinkers of the discipline until quite recently and in the absence of any perceived need to articulate the discipline's contemporary relationship to a changing geo-demography and geo-economy will remain so for the foreseeable future.

Las Vegas: A Venal Example

Las Vegas, perhaps the most unremittingly venal of all cities, due to force of circumstance, has seen fit to comprehensively redevelop its commercial core. In so doing it has become a leader in this form of development, standing as its primary example of an entirely new and commercially provocative 'advance' in architectural production.

Since the 50s fundamental changes have occurred in the marketing of the Vegas casino/hotel to meet this change in demographic patterns. The contraction of the amount individuals are prepared to spend has been associated with a change in the types of visitors themselves. The rise of post-permanent populations, of selective tourist economies, marked the nature of the Vegas economy from the first.[1] Since the 50s, however, the expansion of tourism has made a significant impact on the nature of retailing in major population centres. Vegas has witnessed major transformations in its demographic. More families and foreign tourists have ensured that the classic Vegas casino/hotel has moved into new and more adventurous programmatic experiments. Circus Circus extended the classic Vegas programmatic mix.[2] The once detached event, a Cher concert or a World Boxing Title, for example, was no longer merely contiguous but was now integrated within the gaming plate itself. The event-attractor and the primary programme were now allied for the first time.

Emphasis on geo-demographic and geo-economic data as the foundation for a comprehensive reappraisal of the conditions of urban use can only be broached by architects when they finally deign to accept such data as relevant and present.

The Coincidence of Architectural Theory and Vegas

Certain developments at the theoretical limits of architectural practice have recently come together. Firstly, the wider acceptance of the ideas of Bernard Tschumi, most specifically concerning the reappraisal of an exclusive modernist programmatics, is of primary importance. Tschumi's investigations into what is widely referred to as 'cross-programming', the juxtaposition of otherwise exclusive and antithetical programmes – sky diving in the elevator shaft, roller-skating in the laundromat – provoked not only a reinvigorated interest in programme, per se, but the idea that distinct programmes might be juxtaposed in the same space rather than exclusively preserved in a cellular arrangement.[3] The notion of a broad floor plate, which juxtaposed different programmatic types without separation, now became possible. Speculation concerning an architecture, which might contain this kind of programmatics, has lead to a number of developments that extend the floor slab as a deep plan facility and to its further development in section as a continuous ramped plate unencumbered by fixed vertical circulation.

The interest of practices such as OMA and MRVDV in this approach stems from a coincidence of these issues and has developed into a full blown topological or landscape paradigm in the work of FOA, Jesse Reiser, Stan Allen and latterly Peter Eisenman and Zaha Hadid. What has driven this shift compositionally is a wish to rid the floor plate of all intervening objects, to make of it a flow space constructed from conditions of intra-programmatic flow rather than a space implied by the navigation of fixed objects or ranked cells. Its derivation owes a great deal to the nature of the Vegas casino/hotel and the development of a full-blown event/programme amalgamation. From this perspective architectural planning is no longer concerned with the division of space into discreet and discontinuous entities. Rather this space, which we might call field space for the sake of this argument, has a continuous quality subtending flows, thickenings and areas of high density – it is more like a weather map than a traditional architectural plan.

Additionally field space embraces the homogeneity of globalisation as globalised extension through the figure of the continuous programmable plate.[4] The Vegas casino is its quintessential paradigm. All probable programmes are simultaneously present in one deep space; a field of ubiquitous programmatic inclusions in which everything is simultaneously available on the same surface. The apparent limitlessness of this space, the lack of internal divisions, the remoteness and invisibility of the perimeter container reduces any opportunity to fashion architectural effects to the floor and the ceiling. While the ceiling remains the plane of major spectacle the floor is coded to exaggerate the total spend. In the contemporary Vegas hotel/casino, retail has been comprehensively introduced to the gaming plate. Navigation within the casino floor is now articulated by set piece retail structures offering not only food and refreshment but also branded goods. Within the gaming plate – organised increasingly on a landscape model – the most desirable branded commodities are distributed as brand islands. The architectural organisation of these spatialities has now passed beyond a familiar modernist picturesque vocabulary. The organisation of the multi-programmed plate can no longer be achieved by neo-plastic or classical compositional devices, which have concentrated traditionally on the organisation of objects within an undifferentiated field of space. The organisation of objects as programmatic containers and dividers is now redundant. What this new architecture requires is the inversion of the traditional object/field relationship; moving away from an object-based architecture to one now dominated by field.[5]

The organisational vocabulary of architecture is currently undergoing a dramatic transformation. A new one is emerging having forsaken the articulation of 'objects' in favour of flows, densities, horizons, territories, concentrations, singularities, attractors and so on, a vocabulary which purposively avoids the discontinuities of an objectness and a containing space.

Part Two
A proposed political context to the work of Hawkins\Brown

THE FACT IS, whether we like it or not THE FACT IS, that one can say very little about Hawkins\Brown that has not been said by countless other critics in countless other contexts about countless other architectural practices. The nature of architectural criticism being what it is, the scope for any literary review of built work is more than narrowly confined. But this is really to say much more about criticism than it is to say about the practice of architecture itself.

THE FACT IS, that practice as we know it, is changing. Whether this is for the better or for the worse, this view of its changing relies on a Nietzschean perspectivalism; upon, that is to say, where you're coming from – if you're coming from anywhere at all.

THE FACT IS, that practice, whether it likes it or not, must suffer a change: of necessity. It must become dirtier, that is to say, less artistic, less poisonously self-regarding, less self-absorbed. In the long tradition of the continuing capitalist revolution this is but one more Neue Sachlichkeit, yet one further 'new realism', provoked this time by a burgeoning competition from parallel professional disciplines, such as corporate branding and product design. For too long architecture has retained the haughty distance of pre-monetarist professionalism, knowing best at all times and establishing the terms of doctrinal taste regimes.

THE FACT IS, whether you like it or not, the client knows best at every turn. This is true or you have no work. When I was living in Berlin in the late 90s the state of Brandenburg, and Berlin most especially, adopted the tag line, "The future is female"; a bold and incongruous tag line, declared in English to add to its irony. It signified an intention to develop a more conciliatory, discursive and wholly participatory culture, condition it identified with impending globalisation and with a proleptical future with which it was undoubtedly seen as synonymous.[6] Events such as they have unfolded, have delivered this expectation much as it was conceived. On the ground, issues of partnering, participation and non-confrontational negotiation are being actively supported, not only by the surfeit of advisory material issuing from the Deputy Prime Minister's Office to name but the most powerful and persuasive institutional origin, but also through the declared interests of corporate and private clients.[7]

THE FACT IS, whether you like it or not, this has long been the established practice of other service based professional design concerns. A move away from compulsory competitive tendering towards partner teams, invites, at least on the face of it, an opportunity to build long-term relationships with other members of the design team. Indeed the 'privatisation' of both building control and the proposed 'privatisation' of planning control, offers an opportunity to construct the whole team in a non-adversarial structure giving the client a fuller, more coordinated service.

THE FACT IS, the art of communication is fast becoming the key skill of the architect in this new non-adversarial, affirmative environment. Whether you like it or not, "The future is female"; the future whatever this may mean for a culture always and already immersed in polymorphous and simultaneous futurisms', is always and already present; is preternaturally here, close at hand, offering all that there is to offer, all at once – at the same time. The textures of culture describe not merely a world but all possible worlds.

THE FACT IS, when all worlds are simultaneously present, when all possible commodities have already been formed, fashion plays a discerning role.

THE FACT IS, within this present period of positivism and superficiality; fashion has been recast as a peremptory aspect of the economy. It still harbours those aspects of the culture of capitalism, which made it so reviled by those in the arts who wished for a cultural agenda with a well-defined teleology or end cause. In a culture of simultaneous presence in which the future is diabolically affirmative all aspects of permanence and authenticity have been stripped away.

THE FACT IS, a kind of creative love for commodification illuminates the context of a contemporary architectural practice, caught in the headlights of capitalism's juggernaut. Given the level of productive resources at this moment in the evolution of capitalism, the earth could here and now be paradise. Conversely, the inherent instability of its mechanisms of production, throws this possibility against a latent catastrophe. This petrifying dialectic, has pressed architecture against the strict demands of the latest phase of capitalism.

THE FACT IS, whether you like it or not, plagiarism plays an increasing role in the commodification of architectural production. Now that Local Authorities have seen fit to classify architects as small, medium and signature – a perverse but alarmingly perceptive classification – the possibility of a noteworthy architectural author playing the role of savant within a culture of simultaneous presence, offers as much, or should I say as little, to an overburdened yet uninspired professional practice as it ever did. But things have changed, as you knew they would. There is something positively interesting in plagiarism, but only if one willfully declares it. Not least it is honest without reeking of authenticity; it's economical – why bother inventing when there are perfectly good examples of appropriate solutions already in existence; it's fashionable – probably its most appropriate quality.

THE FACT IS, that which is fashionable is necessarily short-lived, as you knew it would be, and fits itself to the machinations of market capitalism and to those aspects of commodity exchange which determine its duration. What, if anything, can be relevant within fashion to architecture? The question is an enduring one because there is something within the discipline, and to a large extent this is increasing, which lends itself to the fleeting and the diaphanous. Currently there is a trend away from formal preoccupations towards an interest in programmatics. A trend, which is, I have no doubt, a formalism of sorts, but which has nevertheless refocused the debate upon rudely commercial themes.

THE FACT IS, a larger proportion of buildings are the illegitimate progeny of non-believers, undertaken and executed by builders – not by architects, folk who have never aspired to the 'holy qualification' and who do better for it anyway. They are the 80%ters – 80% of the building stock is executed by them. Although this is much lamented by the profession at large it seems to me that there might be some scope for a return to this kind of modesty last seen with the work of the Smithsons.

THE FACT IS, most of the buildings constructed in the general course of events are entirely invisible and more or less without remarkable substance. And you know, this makes me feel good. After too many years of ego architecture the anonymity of 80% building is wholly refreshing. These immodest buildings of illegitimate, even bastard beginnings, are, without exception, pragmatic to the core. They are fit for purpose. This fact alone marks them out as interesting, even vital, against a backdrop of effete plagiarism and painterly formalism.

At a time when difference is being progressively reduced by the indigenous homogenisation of mass culture, and at a time when architecture has ceased to be interested in the nature of diversity in society, as well as in space, it seems altogether pertinent not to say urgent, that a new and more contemporary view might be taken of the Metropolitan context with specific reference to the nature of social space and how it might be constructed within the structures of contemporary market capitalism and its politics.

One thing's for sure, there's got to be new ways of doing things. Perhaps the regressive practices within the profession are structural enough to ensure it will lose market share to a number of other more modern and more 'female' enterprises. As it is, from the perspective of old school form makers, precisely those who love the way they are architects, the way they deport themselves as architects, very little will change and consequently even less will be left to base pertinent work upon.

There is something unsullied in pragmatics, unblemished, perhaps blameless, which has been ignored for far too long. In the doctrine of form to function whatever the dismissals of the last years, there remains an opportunity to discard the irrelevance of ego-narcissism and to build a new programmatics based on social use. Contemporary information culture has restored the opportunities of mass observation without the cost and made geo-demographic information generally available to architects over the wire. A carpet of abstract data now covers little England at some considerable depth, revealing every lifestyle habit and inadvertency. Its overwhelming presence demands a consequent plurality, making it difficult, in the face of the body democratic, to venture into self-serving poetries.

A Weak Architecture
This re-focusing constructs an architecture of what could be termed WEAK FORM, precisely a WEAK ARCHITECTURE disinterested in the resisting and closed geometries of the Miesian aesthetic paradigm; an architecture driven by a much more flexible response to programme. Pleural, inclusive, complex and formally pliable, such an approach constructs an architecture based on the needs of a broadening and more variegated social mix. It does so in terms of the conditions of an unprecedented social mobility, which itself establishes a relevant aesthetic, formulated from these conditions on the basis of an inventive economy and practical execution.

What is left is a kind of compliance, an acceptance of the pragmatic terms of the everyday and the materially real. What might be constructed is a compliant and weak architecture forged from a programmatic intelligence sporting an unapologetic social agenda.

City populations are composed increasingly from both permanent and transitory populations. The expansion of tourism in recent decades has seriously affected the populations of major cities influencing and distorting their peculiar economies. Contemporary urban economics is based in part on these phenomena.

Circus Circus featured trapeze circus acts performing above the heads of the gamblers over the casino floor.

See Tschumi's Architecture and Disjunction, Cambridge, MA: MIT Press, 1994.

The web has created a dramatic transformation in the nature of commerce, most especially and most importantly for architecture in the area of retail. The nature of urban retail outlets, the way they are organised and the way they present commodities for sale is undergoing a number of dramatic transformations. The appearance of web retail has constituted a reorganisation of traditional divisions within the global marketplace and forced their reorganisation. The most dramatic is the association of the retail and leisure industries. The recent Time, Warner, AOL, EMI mergers has seen the creation of the first global, retail/entertainment conglomerate which has the facility to provide publishing, cinema and popular music to a huge number of Internet users. At a market value of some $2,000 billion US it has a capitalisation of twice the size of the UK's current GDP (gross domestic product). The purchasing power of such a capital rich leviathan and its interest in pressing home a global brand image behind its ubiquitous web presence makes large sections of the world's hyper-cities – Paris, London, New York, Tokyo – vulnerable to its territorialisation. Not only is it entirely possible for such a commercial phenomenon to territorialise large areas of the central districts of these cities it is already underway. Nike Town is a branded neighbourhood, a kind of forerunner of a comprehensive branded district in which tens of blocks of mid-town Manhattan, for example, could be assimilated and dedicated to the retail of a single conglomerate brand.

[5]The predominant compositional paradigm of twentieth century modernism depends upon the association of abstract objects or figures displaced against and contrasted with a neutral, non-figured, empty background. It is a play of the presence and absence of graphical objects within the perimeter of the drawing plane or the canvas – a juxtaposition of the configured object constructed in contradistinction to an undifferentiated and receding background; what has come to be known as a figure/ ground or object/ field opposition. OBJECT is defined as a form, or collection of forms that sustains identifiable figuration in contrast to an undifferentiated, formless background. This back-ground, the FIELD, surrounds and delimits distinct objects with a continuous and, most importantly, non-perspectival space. The difference between object and field is one of relative quality and extension. A field remains a field only insofar as it can be clearly discerned as that which is not the object and vice-versa. But within the limits of the drawing plane objects and fields maintain a degree of interchangeability, which is both telescopic and hierarchical, connoting primary, secondary and tertiary strategraphical levels of complexity. Objects, which have significant extensions within a primary field constitute secondary fields when smaller objects are superimposed upon them. They act as fields to these smaller groupings in the same way as the drawing plane constitutes an ultimate field within which the most extended objects of the composition are delineated. This hierarchical interchange is, clearly, infinitely extendable.

[6]Prolepsis is that intellectual mechanism by means of which a presumed future is treated as already present.

[7]Following the Latham report in 1994 (Constructing the Team) and more pertinently the Egan Report of 1998 (Rethinking Construction), proactive approaches to the reorganisation of working methods in practice have been sought. Against the recommendations of the central government initiative 'M4I' practices have been encouraged to establish a culture of performance placing emphasis on the organisation and management of the construction process. From an early stage issues of sustainability and 'respect for people' are promoted in the context of client requirements.

WOULD YOU RATHER HAVE A ROAD, BRIDGE OR BUILDING NAMED AFTER YOU?

THIS BOOK WILL NOT HELP YOU FALL IN LOVE, BUT MAY BOOST YOUR LIBIDO A LITTLE.

9
alsoness

Birmingham Institute of Art & Design

Complete transformation of the interiors of a Sixties building to create a new social heart to the art school Campus.

too is not a negative;
too is as well;
too is I didn't think of that;
too is can we really;
too is and it doesn't cost anymore[1];
too is two birds one stone;
too is seeing the happy accident;
too is one and one makes three;

[1] Birmingham Institute of Art & Design;
New window system;
Didn't cost the £2m they expected;

from the Women's Pioneer Centre;
spawned Bethnal Green Road;
fed Maggie's Centre;
added Trowbridge Centre;
a lot of centres;
and Woodley besides;
back to Bethnal;
led to Bury St Edmunds house;
what's more Hope Sufferance Wharf;
furthermore Hertford Road;
Billiard Hall to boot;
moreover Heddon St in 96;
above and beyond the soho trilogy;
adding Henry Moore Foundation;
plus Roald Dahl and Bradbury St;
likewise Stamford Works and Hackney College;
and so on';

The first shed on Mars 2010-ish

children love the word and;
so do we;
everything's an encore;
a client deserves as much;
they're paying;
we should transcend their expectations[1];
leave them feeling full of and;
out of breath;
like a child telling a story;
and isn't and fantastic;

[1]University of Central England;
Simple repair job grew;
Became vibrant new architectural vision for art school;

START A PETITION TO DEMOLISH A BUILDING YOU LOATHE.

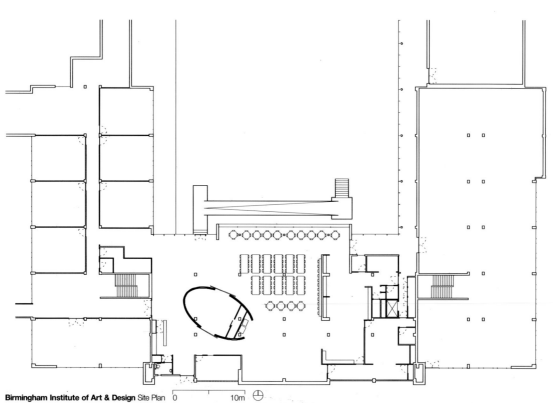

Birmingham Institute of Art & Design Site Plan